The One with All the
RECIPES

An Unofficial Cookbook
for Fans of Friends

TERESA FINNEY

ULYSSES PRESS

Published in the United States by:
ULYSSES PRESS
P.O. Box 3440
Berkeley, CA 94703
www.ulyssespress.com

ISBN: 978-1-61243-864-1
Library of Congress Control Number: 2018954474

Printed in the United States by Versa Press
10 9 8 7 6 5 4

Acquisitions editor: Bridget Thoreson
Managing editor: Claire Chun
Editor: Susan Lang
Proofreader: Barbara Schultz
Front cover design: Malea Clark-Nicholson
Interior design and production: what!design @ whatweb.com
Cover artwork from shutterstock.com: skyline © Andrey Bayda; couch © Nattstudio; roasted chicken and meatball sub © Brent Hofacker; milkshakes © Africa Studio
Interior photos: see page 151

CONTENTS

INTRODUCTION 5

APPETIZERS, SALADS, AND SIDES 7

Cheese Plate 9
Salmon Rillettes 11
Creamy Artichoke Dip. 13
Double Date Chicken Wings 15
Sweet Potato and Marshmallow Casserole 17
Fabulous French Fries. 19
Diet-Breaking Garlic Bread 21
Curry Dip with Crudités 23

Onion Tartlets 25
Simple Garden Salad 27
Thanksgiving Yams 29
On the Side Caesar Salad 31
Fried Stuff with Cheese. 33
Couscous with Pine Nuts and Golden Raisins 35
Breakup Jam 37

BRUNCH & LUNCH 38

Brunch Bagel with Cream Cheese, Tomato, and Cucumbers 39
Banana Nut Muffins 41
Classic Ham and Cheese Quiche 43
Stupid British Snack Food Scones 45
Soap Opera Turkey Sandwich 46

Grandma's Inappropriate Chicken Salad 47
Creamy and Cool Cucumber Soup. 49
Acting Lines Noodle Soup 51
All-Time Favorite Meatball Sub. 53
Thanksgiving Leftovers Sandwich 55

DINNER 56

Steaks and an Eggplant 57
Kiddie Mac and Cheese 59
Thanksgiving Turkey for One. 61
Chicken Pox Spaghetti and Salad 62
Turkey Burgers .65

Political Commentator Mushroom, Green Pepper, and Onion Pizza 67
Funeral Reception Honey-Glazed Ham. 69
TV Dinner Pigs in a Blanket 71
Grilled Cheese and All That 73

Two Chicks Chicken Breasts 75

Jewelry Box Mac and Cheese 77

California Roll. 78

Special Pizzas 81

Better than Takeout Fried Chicken. 82

Engagement Ring Lasagna. 84

Ground Beef Tacos. 87

Spicy Enchiladas 88

Birthday Party Hamburgers
and Coleslaw 90

Top-Notch Tomato Sauce. 93

Critical Parents Spaghetti. 95

Scandalous Mom Kung Pao
Chicken 97

Sizzling Fajitas 99

Breakup Pizza 101

Ponzu Ginger Shrimp Ravioli 103

Steak Fried Rice 104

Until the Cheese Bubbles Vegetarian
Lasagna 107

DESSERTS 109

All-Occasion Vanilla Cake. 110

Memorable Kiwi-Lime Pie 113

Fudgy Chocolate Brownies 115

"French Aunt" Chocolate Chip
Cookies. 117

Divorced Parents Pumpkin Pie 119

Perfect Pox Peach Cobbler 120

Best Oatmeal Raisin Cookies Ever 123

Fake Chocolate Cake with
Cranberry Frosting 125

Christmas Caramel Candies 127

Fabulous Flan 129

Chocolate Mousse 131

Thanksgiving Trifle 132

Floor Cheesecake. 134

Mad, Sad, and Glad Chocolate
Donuts 136

DRINKS 138

The Cape Codder 139

No-Faux Hot Chocolate 141

Not-so-Fine Margaritas 142

Monica's Ceiling Banana Smoothie 143

Spiced Cider 145

Fun Irish Coffee 147

Tiki Death Punch 148

Vacay Mimosas .149

Strawberry Milkshake 150

PHOTO CREDITS. 151

ABOUT THE AUTHOR .152

INTRODUCTION

• • •

For a woman in her mid-30s, television from the '90s tends to evoke feelings of nostalgia. Thanks to internet streaming, those television memories from childhood can easily be revisited. From 1994 to 2004, *Friends* was as much a part of my weekly life as studying for algebra tests and learning how to drive on the 101. The show debuted when I was in the fourth grade and had its series finale two years after I graduated high school, so it was a big part of the culture that surrounded me as both a kid and a teenager. Like lots of people who loved television in the '90s, I would plop down in front of the TV set with whatever dinner my mom whipped up that night and enjoy the antics of Rachel, Monica, Phoebe, Ross, Chandler, and Joey.

One of my favorite things about *Friends* was the way food acted as a supporting character and an underlying theme. This was thanks—at least in part—to Monica Geller working in the food industry. Whether Monica was moonlighting as a wedding caterer or enlisting the help of her buddies in getting Thanksgiving dinner on the table (and there are so many great Thanksgiving-themed episodes), show writers were able to inject food into countless episodes. And they did so brilliantly, from the very first season with Rachel digging into a lasagna to fish out her engagement ring, to Ross describing how to keep a turkey sandwich moist, to Phoebe's grandmother trying to pass off her chocolate chip cookie recipe as a family heirloom when, in fact, it came from the back of a chocolate chip bag.

For this book, I created recipes inspired by various food-themed *Friends* episodes, scenes, and one-liners. You'll find cocktails and drinks like Fun Irish Coffee and Tiki Death Punch, appetizers like a Cheese Plate (with "milk that you chew"), and main courses like Spicy

Enchiladas (that might even induce labor!). I'd never forget about dessert, so I included recipes for Divorced Parents Pumpkin Pie and, of course, Floor Cheesecake.

I think these recipes will be great for people who are *Friends* fanatics as well as people who have never watched the show. Whether you're preparing an appetizer for a chill Sunday night dinner or throwing a massive *Friends*-themed party, these recipes will, as they say, be there for you.

APPETIZERS, SALADS, AND SIDES

CHEESE PLATE

Here's a cheese plate made with "milk that you chew." We recommend pairing with a nice sliced baguette, but crackers will work as well—just as long as you have something. Your cheese needs a buddy, after all.

Yield: 4 servings • *Prep time:* 10 minutes

1 (8½-ounce) baguette, sliced
3 tablespoons extra-virgin olive oil
8 ounces aged cheddar, sliced thinly
8 ounces smoked Gouda, sliced thinly

4 ounces goat cheese, softened
4-ounce Gorgonzola wedge
⅓ cup apricot jam
¼ cup spicy brown mustard

1. Set your oven to broil or to 400°F. Arrange the baguette slices in a single layer on a medium baking sheet. Drizzle the extra-virgin olive oil over the baguette slices and toast in the oven for about 3 minutes, or until the baguette slices have become golden brown. Set aside.

2. On a large wooden cutting board arrange the sliced cheddar and smoked Gouda around the corners. Arrange the softened goat cheese and the Gorgonzola wedge directly on the cutting board. Spoon the jams and mustard into small serving bowls. Place the baguette slices in the center of the board, then position the jams and mustard around the board.

3. Serve immediately.

SALMON RILLETTES

When hosting a poker party, don't forget the essentials: chips, nuts, guacamole, and, of course, salmon rillettes, a high-class snack for a high-stakes game. Am I right?

Yield: 4 servings • *Prep time:* 10 minutes • *Cook time:* 15 minutes

10 baguette slices

2 tablespoons extra-virgin olive oil

2 cups dry white wine

1 tablespoon roughly chopped shallot (about ½ small shallot)

1 pound salmon fillet, cut into 1-inch pieces

½ cup mayonnaise

2 tablespoons thinly sliced fresh chives

juice of 1 small lemon

1 teaspoon kosher salt

1 teaspoon freshly ground black pepper

1. Set your oven to broil or to 400°F. Arrange the baguette slices in a single layer on a medium baking sheet. Drizzle the extra-virgin olive oil over the baguette slices and toast in the oven for about 3 minutes, or until the baguette slices have become golden brown. Set aside.

2. In a medium saucepan set over medium heat, bring the wine and shallot to a gentle boil, about 10 minutes. Reduce the heat to low and add the salmon pieces.

3. Gently poach the salmon for 5 minutes, or until the centers of the fish are just barely opaque. Drain the poaching liquid through a fine-mesh strainer and reserve the shallot. Place the salmon and shallot in a large bowl.

4. To the bowl with the salmon and shallot, add the mayonnaise, fresh chives, and lemon juice. Gently stir with a rubber spatula just to combine, being sure not to overmix. Season with the salt and black pepper.

5. Transfer the mixture to a small serving bowl and serve with baguette slices.

CREAMY ARTICHOKE DIP

Who doesn't love an artichoke dip at a fancy New Year's Eve party? There's at least one Janice in New York who goes crazy for it. Serve this dip with a vegetable tray, crunchy pita chips, or baguette slices and you'll have all your guests exclaiming, "Oh my God!"

Yield: 8 servings • *Prep time:* 10 minutes • *Cook time:* 30 to 35 minutes

2 (14-ounce) cans artichoke hearts, rinsed, drained, and coarsely chopped

½ cup mayonnaise

¼ cup plus 1 tablespoon grated Parmesan cheese

1 tablespoon freshly squeezed lemon juice

2 cloves garlic, finely minced

2 scallions, roughly chopped

salt and pepper, to taste

1. Preheat the oven to 425°F.

2. In the bowl of a food processor, place half the artichokes along with the mayonnaise, ¼ cup of the Parmesan, and the lemon juice and garlic. Process until smooth.

3. Add the chopped scallions and the remaining artichokes, and continue to process just a second or two more.

4. Transfer the dip to a 1-quart baking dish and sprinkle the remaining Parmesan on top.

5. Bake for 30 to 35 minutes, or until golden brown and bubbling. Serve immediately.

DOUBLE DATE CHICKEN WINGS

If you've ever been on a double date with your friend where you were scheming to break up the other couple, you'll know these chicken wings will come in handy. That is, as long as the couple aren't related and one of them eats like a weasel!

Yield: 2 servings • *Prep time:* 15 minutes • *Cook time:* 45 minutes

3 tablespoons unsalted butter, melted
⅓ cup all-purpose flour
1 tablespoon paprika
1 teaspoon kosher salt

1 teaspoon garlic salt
1 teaspoon freshly ground black pepper
½ teaspoon cayenne pepper
10 chicken wings, thawed and tips removed

1. Preheat the oven to 425°F.

2. Line a large rimmed baking sheet with aluminum foil and brush the foil with the melted butter. Set aside.

3. Using a paper towel, pat dry the chicken wings to remove any extra moisture and for even browning in the oven.

4. To a large zip-top freezer bag, add the flour, paprika, salt, garlic salt, black pepper, and cayenne pepper, and shake well to combine. Add the chicken wings and shake well to distribute the seasonings evenly.

5. Place the chicken wings in a single layer on the prepared baking sheet. Bake for 30 minutes.

6. After 30 minutes, turn wings over with tongs and bake for an additional 15 minutes, or until golden brown and crispy.

SWEET POTATO AND MARSHMALLOW CASSEROLE

This southern staple casserole will deliver on gooey deliciousness even if you don't arrange the marshmallows in concentric circles. It is a perfect dish for your first Friendsgiving.

Yield: 8 servings • *Prep time:* 25 minutes • *Cook time:* 20 minutes

8 medium sweet potatoes, peeled and cut into ½-inch cubes

½ cup whole milk

4 tablespoons (½ stick) unsalted butter

½ teaspoon ground nutmeg

1 teaspoon kosher salt, plus more for salting water

1 teaspoon freshly ground black pepper

2 cups marshmallows

1. Preheat the oven to 375°F.

2. Place sweet potatoes in a large saucepan and cover them with water. Salt the pot generously and then set the saucepan over medium heat and bring to a boil. Reduce the heat, and let simmer until the sweet potatoes are easily pierced with a fork, about 20 minutes. Drain and return the sweet potatoes to the saucepan.

3. Add the milk, butter, and ground nutmeg to the saucepan, and mash the mixture with a potato masher. Mash until smooth, then season with salt and black pepper.

4. Transfer to a 2-quart baking dish and top with the marshmallows.

5. Bake for 20 minutes, or until the center is warmed through and the marshmallows have browned slightly. Remove from the oven and serve warm.

FABULOUS FRENCH FRIES

It's really up to you whether to share these fries or not. (I know a guy who wouldn't.) But in case you do, this recipe will feed four and can be whipped up pretty quickly.

Yield: 4 servings • *Prep time:* 45 minutes • *Cook time:* 20 minutes

4 large russet potatoes, cut into ¼-inch sticks

2–3 quarts vegetable oil

salt and pepper, to taste

1. Line a large baking sheet with paper towels.

2. Soak the potato sticks in cold water for 20 minutes. Drain and rinse, then let dry on the paper towel–lined baking sheet.

3. Heat the oil in a large pot or Dutch oven over medium-high heat until the oil registers 330°F on a fry thermometer.

4. Paper towel-dry the potatoes one last time. Working in batches, drop the potato sticks into the hot oil, making sure not to overcrowd the pot. Stir the fries using a large slotted spoon or kitchen skimmer until they just begin to soften, 3 to 4 minutes. You should be able to fry all the potatoes in about three batches.

5. Remove the first batch of fries and let drain on the paper towel–lined baking sheet. Immediately sprinkle with salt and black pepper.

6. Repeat steps 4 and 5 with the remaining potato sticks.

7. Bring the oil temperature up to 360°F. Working in batches again, drop the fries back into the oil for a second fry. Cook just until golden brown and crispy, 2 to 3 minutes. (Remove any fries that turn brown too quickly.) Sprinkle with more salt and black pepper immediately after removing from the oil. Serve hot.

DIET-BREAKING GARLIC BREAD

You'll want to keep this delicious side dish away from anyone's little sister who may have a garlic bread weakness. Unless she once made a move on your ex, in which case, garlic breath is a fitting punishment.

Yield: 4 to 6 servings • *Prep time:* 5 minutes • *Cook time:* 5 minutes

8 ounces sourdough bread loaf, cut in half lengthwise and then cut into sliced ½-inch slices

2½ tablespoons extra virgin olive oil

3 tablespoons unsalted butter, melted

2 teaspoons garlic powder

1 teaspoon freshly ground black pepper

2 ounces Parmesan cheese, grated

1. Preheat the broiler to its high setting or set oven temperature to 400°F.

2. Line a large baking sheet with aluminum foil and arrange the sourdough slices on it. Drizzle the extra virgin olive oil over the bread slices.

3. In a small mixing bowl, whisk the melted butter, garlic powder, and black pepper to combine. Using a pastry brush, brush a little of the garlic butter mixture on each slice of sourdough. Sprinkle Parmesan on each slice.

4. Toast the bread for 5 minutes, or until it is golden brown and the Parmesan has crisped. Serve immediately.

CURRY DIP WITH CRUDITÉS

If your parents drop by for dinner unannounced, you'll be sure to impress them with this amazing curry dip. It might not be enough to win favorite-child status, but it is a step in the right direction! Serve with a tray of raw vegetables.

Yield: 1½ cups • *Prep time:* 10 minutes

½ cup full-fat sour cream

¼ cup mayonnaise

3 ounces full-fat cream cheese, room temperature

1 teaspoon fresh lemon juice

1 teaspoon curry powder

½ teaspoon ground cumin

½ teaspoon kosher salt

¼ teaspoon turmeric

⅓ cup finely chopped celery (about 1 rib)

½ large cucumber, seeded and finely chopped

1 scallion, trimmed and finely chopped

1. In a small mixing bowl, whisk the sour cream, mayonnaise, cream cheese, lemon juice, curry powder, ground cumin, salt, and turmeric just to combine. Right before serving, stir in the celery, cucumber, and scallion with a rubber spatula.

2. Pour the dip into a serving bowl.

ONION TARTLETS

These onion tartlets are a good distraction for any potential employers who happen to have the munchies. They make a great follow up if you're still hungry after the Ponzu Ginger Shrimp Ravioli on page 103!

Yield: 9 tartlets • *Prep time:* 55 minutes • *Cook time:* 30 minutes

2 tablespoons extra virgin olive oil

3 sweet onions such as Vidalia

½ teaspoon kosher salt, to taste

¼ cup vegetable stock

8 ounces goat cheese, room temperature

1 teaspoon freshly ground black pepper

1 sheet frozen puff pastry

½ tablespoon roughly chopped fresh thyme

1. To a medium skillet set over medium heat, drizzle in the olive oil and add the diced onions. Sprinkle in the salt and stir occasionally. After 5 minutes, pour in the vegetable stock and stir. Reduce the heat to low and let the onions cook until caramelized, about 25 to 30 minutes.

2. Remove the onions from the heat and set aside to cool completely.

3. In a small mixing bowl, combine the goat cheese and black pepper. Mix well using a rubber spatula. Set aside.

4. Preheat the oven to 375°F. Line a large baking sheet with parchment paper.

5. Unroll the defrosted puff pastry and place on the baking sheet. Spread the goat cheese evenly over the entire sheet of puff pastry, leaving a ½-inch border on all sides. Spoon the caramelized onions evenly on top of the goat cheese and sprinkle with the fresh thyme.

6. Bake for 25 to 30 minutes, or until golden.

7. Let cool for 10 minutes, then slice into approximately 2 x 3-inch tartlets.

8. Serve immediately.

SIMPLE GARDEN SALAD

Here's an uncomplicated garden salad for any occasion, even a blind date. Just make sure your friend is willing to share meals if you want a call back.

Yield: 4 servings • *Prep time:* 10 minutes

For the vinaigrette:

2 tablespoons white wine vinegar

1 tablespoon Dijon mustard

¼ teaspoon kosher salt

¼ teaspoon freshly ground black pepper

pinch of sugar

¼ cup extra virgin olive oil

For the salad:

3–4 cups chopped romaine, rinsed and dried

½ cup grape tomatoes

½ cucumber, thinly sliced into half-moons

4 scallions, finely chopped

2 radishes, thinly sliced

1 carrot, peeled and thinly sliced

salt and pepper, to taste

1. Make the vinaigrette: In a small mixing bowl, whisk the vinegar, mustard, kosher salt, black pepper, and sugar. Slowly drizzle in the olive oil until dressing has emulsified, or come together.

2. In a large mixing bowl, place the romaine, tomatoes, cucumber, scallions, radishes, and carrots then drizzle in the prepared dressing.

3. Season with salt and pepper, toss the salad, and serve immediately.

THANKSGIVING YAMS

You will love this dish. Yams are a good source of complex carbohydrates so unless they are your worst enemy (the other to remain unnamed), go ahead and enjoy!

Yield: 4 servings • *Prep time:* 7 minutes • *Cook time:* 50 to 60 minutes

4 garnet yams
2 tablespoons granulated sugar
1 tablespoon light brown sugar

1 ½ teaspoons ground cinnamon
4 tablespoons store-bought unsalted whipped butter

1. Preheat the oven to 400°F.

2. Line a large baking sheet with aluminum foil and set aside.

3. In a small mixing bowl, whisk both sugars and the ground cinnamon to combine. Set aside.

4. Pierce each yam in several places and place on the prepared baking sheet.

5. Bake the yams for 40 minutes, then sprinkle the sugar and cinnamon mixture evenly on top of each yam.

6. Continue to bake for an additional 10 to 20 minutes, or until tender.

7. Remove yams from oven and let cool slightly. Using a small knife, cut a slit into each of the yams. Pinch the ends of the yams, exposing the flesh, and drop a tablespoon of whipped butter into each yam.

8. Serve immediately.

ON THE SIDE CAESAR SALAD

This classic Caesar salad is fresh and delicious and hearty enough to be a full meal—which is especially great if you're trying to watch your spending. Just make sure the rest of your group gets the memo so they don't try to make you split the bill for their more expensive tastes!

Yield: 1 large serving • *Prep time:* 5 minutes • *Cook time:* 5 minutes

2 slices sourdough bread, cut into 1-inch cubes

¼ cup extra virgin olive oil

½ small head romaine lettuce, torn into ½-inch pieces

2 tablespoons store-bought Caesar salad dressing, or to taste

2 tablespoons grated Parmesan cheese

kosher salt, to taste

¼ teaspoon freshly cracked black pepper

1. Set your oven to its high broiler setting, or preheat the oven to 400°F. Line a small baking sheet with aluminum foil. Place the cubes of sourdough bread on the baking sheet and drizzle with the olive oil. Toast for 5 minutes, or until browned to your preference. Remove from the oven and let cool.

2. To a medium mixing bowl, add the torn romaine pieces. Pour in the dressing and the Parmesan cheese. Toss with tongs.

3. Season with salt and black pepper, and serve immediately.

FRIED STUFF WITH CHEESE

These homemade mozzarella sticks make a fun weeknight snack, should you daydream about marrying your fried cheese–loving best friend.

Yield: 2 to 4 servings • *Prep time:* 35 minutes • *Cook time:* 3 to 6 minutes

1 large egg

1 tablespoon milk

½ cup all-purpose flour

½ teaspoon seasoned salt

¾ cup panko breadcrumbs

1 teaspoon kosher salt, plus more if desired for the fried sticks

1 teaspoon freshly cracked black pepper

8 ounces mozzarella, cut into ½-thick sticks

vegetable oil, for frying

marinara sauce, to serve

1. In a small bowl, whisk the egg and milk to combine. In a small shallow dish, whisk the flour and seasoned salt to combine. In another small shallow dish, whisk together the breadcrumbs, salt, and black pepper.

2. Keeping one hand dry, dip one mozzarella stick into the egg mixture, then into the flour mixture. Dip the stick back into the egg mixture, then dunk it into the breadcrumb mixture. Repeat this step for an extra crispy mozzarella stick. Set the breaded mozzarella stick on a small sheet pan. Repeat with the remaining cheese sticks (you should be able to fry all cheese sticks in three batches).

3. Chill the breaded cheese sticks in the refrigerator for at least 30 minutes.

4. In a 10-inch cast-iron skillet set over medium-high heat, pour in the vegetable oil to about 2-inches deep. Bring oil to 350°F on a fry thermometer. Working in batches, drop the cheese sticks into the oil and let fry for 1 to 2 minutes. Don't let the cheese melt.

5. Transfer the fried cheese sticks to a paper towel–lined plate and sprinkle with additional salt, if desired.

6. Serve hot with a side of store-bought marinara sauce. You can also serve the fried cheese with a side of French fries.

COUSCOUS WITH PINE NUTS AND GOLDEN RAISINS

A couscous good enough to eat on your date with an Eastern European UN diplomat, which is perhaps something his interpreter could convey for you.

Yield: 4 servings • *Prep time:* 15 minutes • *Cook time:* 25 minutes

2 cups vegetable stock

1 cup uncooked couscous

2 tablespoons extra virgin olive oil

1 bunch scallions, thinly sliced (both white and green parts)

½ cup pine nuts

½ cup golden raisins

salt and pepper, to taste

1. In a medium saucepan set over medium-high heat, bring the vegetable stock to a boil. Turn off the heat and immediately stir in the couscous. Cover and let stand in the saucepan until the liquid is fully absorbed, 5 to 7 minutes.

2. Meanwhile, heat a small skillet over medium heat. Add the scallions and pine nuts, and cook until the scallions soften and the nuts give off a fragrant aroma, about 5 minutes.

3. Fluff the couscous with a fork. Add the scallions and pine nuts mixture and the golden raisins, stirring to combine. Season with salt and pepper. Serve warm.

BREAKUP JAM

This sweet strawberry jam would be a nice gift for a friend who just went through a break up (or who is on a break). In happier times, this makes for a delicious movie theater snack—just bring a little spoon!

Yield: 1¾ cups • *Prep time:* 15 minutes • *Cook time:* 10 minutes

16 ounces fresh strawberries, hulled
½ cup granulated sugar
juice of 2 small lemons, about ¼ cup

1. Place the strawberries in the bowl of a food processor and pulse until finely chopped. Transfer to a medium saucepan, and stir in the sugar and lemon juice with a wooden spatula or wooden spoon.

2. Stirring frequently, cook over medium-high heat until the jam has thickened and is bubbling, about 10 minutes.

3. Remove from the heat and let cool just slightly in the saucepan, 5 minutes. Transfer to a glass jar and let cool completely at room temperature.

4. Cover and store in the refrigerator for up to 10 days.

BRUNCH
& LUNCH

● ● ●

BRUNCH BAGEL WITH CREAM CHEESE, TOMATO, AND CUCUMBERS

This is a perfect breakfast inspired by the greatest city in the world. And, as a bonus, it is pretty low-cost, too, which is great in case you're spending all your money on an apartment that you definitely still can't afford.

Yield: 1 • *Prep time:* 5 minutes • *Cook time:* 2 minutes

1 plain bagel

2 heaping tablespoons scallion cream cheese

1 small Roma tomato, sliced

½ medium cucumber, sliced

1. Slice the bagel in half, and toast both halves.

2. Spread 1 heaping tablespoon of cream cheese on each half, arrange the tomato and cucumber slices, and serve.

BANANA NUT MUFFINS

If there's only one banana nut muffin left at your favorite New York City coffee shop, you can make some at home. These also make great freebies for any lovely ladies who may, or may not, be celebrating their birthday.

Yield: 12 muffins • *Prep time:* 15 minutes • *Cook time:* 22 minutes

2 cups whole wheat flour

½ cup old-fashioned rolled oats

2 teaspoons ground cinnamon

1 ½ teaspoons baking soda

½ teaspoon salt

1 ¼ cups mashed banana (about 3 medium very ripe bananas)

3 large eggs

⅓ cup vegetable oil

⅓ cup honey

¼ cup whole milk

1 teaspoon vanilla extract

½ cup chopped walnuts

1. Preheat the oven to 450°F. Line a 12-cup muffin pan with paper baking cups.

2. In a large bowl, whisk the whole wheat flour, rolled oats, ground cinnamon, baking soda, and salt to combine.

3. To the bowl of a stand mixer, or a medium mixing bowl if using a hand mixer, add the mashed bananas. With the mixer set to medium speed, crack in the eggs, and pour in the vegetable oil, honey, milk, and vanilla extract. Combine thoroughly.

4. Pour the wet ingredients into the dry ingredients and stir with a rubber spatula. Fold in the chopped walnuts.

5. Spoon the batter into the prepared muffin pan, filling all the way to the top of each paper baking cup. Bake for 5 minutes at 450°F, then reduce the temperature to 350°F and bake for an additional 16 to 17 minutes, or until a toothpick inserted into the center comes out clean of crumbs.

CLASSIC HAM AND CHEESE QUICHE

Fret not! There is not a single press-on fingernail to be found in this quiche. It's just a bit of sautéed ham and Swiss cheese in a buttery, flaky pie crust that's sure to impress the most critical of moms. Then again, just in case something does go wrong, best to have a back up lasagna in the freezer. Perhaps the vegetarian one on page 107!

Yield: 8 servings • *Prep time:* 20 minutes • *Cook time:* 45 to 55 minutes
• *Chill time:* 20 to 30 minutes

1 (9-inch) deep-dish frozen pie crust

4 ounces ham steak, diced into ½-inch cubes (about ½ cup)

4 large eggs

½ cup whole milk

1 teaspoon fresh oregano, finely chopped (optional)

½ cup shredded Swiss cheese

salt and pepper, to taste

1. Preheat the oven to 400°F.

2. Parbake the frozen pie crust according to package directions.

3. In a skillet set over medium heat, sauté the diced ham just until the edges begin to lightly brown, about 5 minutes. Remove from the heat.

4. In a mixing bowl, whisk together the eggs, milk, salt and pepper, and the fresh oregano (if using) just to combine.

5. Spoon the sautéed ham onto the bottom of the parbaked pie crust, and sprinkle the shredded Swiss cheese on top. Pour in the egg mixture.

6. Bake for 45 to 55 minutes, or until the center of the quiche is no longer jiggly and the top has browned.

7. Allow to cool for 20 to 30 minutes before slicing and serving.

STUPID BRITISH SNACK FOOD SCONES

We all have tough times. Sometimes it just hasn't been your day, but other times you discover your ex is getting remarried. Try not to smash these scones with your hand on one of those days. These sweet, sturdy pastries deserve better. By-the-by, they taste even better when dunked into a mug of hot coffee.

Yield: 8 scones • *Prep time:* 15 minutes • *Bake time:* 25 minutes

2 cups all-purpose flour, plus more for work surface

2½ teaspoons baking powder

1 teaspoon ground cinnamon

½ teaspoon kosher salt

½ cup (1 stick) unsalted butter, chilled

½ cup heavy cream, plus 2 tablespoons for brushing

½ cup light brown sugar

1 large egg, room temperature

1 teaspoon vanilla extract

1 cup mini semi-sweet chocolate chips

1. Preheat the oven to 400°F. Line a large baking sheet with parchment paper.

2. In a large mixing bowl, whisk the flour, baking powder, ground cinnamon, and salt to combine. Using a box grater, grate the butter into the dry ingredients, then toss with either your hands or a fork to combine.

3. In a small mixing bowl, add ½ cup heavy cream along with the brown sugar, egg, and vanilla extract, and whisk to combine.

4. Pour the liquid mixture into the flour mixture and stir with a rubber spatula to combine. Fold in the chocolate chips.

5. Work the dough into a ball and transfer to a lightly floured work surface. Press the dough into an 8-inch circle about 1 inch thick. Cut eight triangles from the dough and place them 2 inches apart on the prepared baking sheet.

6. Brush the scones with the remaining heavy cream and bake for 25 minutes, or until golden brown with edges just slightly crispy.

SOAP OPERA TURKEY SANDWICH

This would be a nice sandwich to have for lunch while you watch one of your best friends make his daytime television acting debut.

Yield: 1 serving • *Prep time:* 5 minutes

2 slices whole grain bread

1 tablespoon mayonnaise

½ tablespoon spicy mustard

2 romaine lettuce leaves

4–6 ounces sliced turkey meat

4 ounces sliced Havarti cheese

1. Lay out the two slices of bread. Spread half of the mayonnaise first and then half of the spicy mustard on each slice.

2. On one slice of bread, place the lettuce leaves and top with the turkey slices. Place the cheese slices on the turkey and top with the other slice of bread. Slice diagonally.

GRANDMA'S INAPPROPRIATE CHICKEN SALAD

How you doin'? Yes, I'm talking to this delicious chicken salad, looking good enough to eat! This is a perfect recipe for that friend we all have who insists he can make anything sound sexy.

Yield: 2 servings • *Prep time:* 10 minutes

2 cups diced rotisserie chicken

¼ cup finely minced red onion

2 heaping tablespoons finely minced celery

2 teaspoons roughly chopped fresh parsley

2 teaspoons freshly squeezed lemon juice

2–3 heaping tablespoons mayonnaise

½ tablespoon Dijon mustard

2 teaspoons kosher salt

2 teaspoons freshly ground black pepper

1. In a medium mixing bowl, combine all ingredients except the salt and pepper.

2. Using a rubber spatula, toss the ingredients to fully combine. Season with the salt and pepper, and toss once more.

3. Spread the chicken salad on whole grain bread for a sandwich or scoop it on top of mixed greens for a carb-free option.

CREAMY AND COOL CUCUMBER SOUP

This chilled cucumber soup could be there to comfort you, should you grow tired of ordering the least expensive thing on the menu when out to dinner with friends.

Yield: 6 servings • *Prep time:* 35 minutes • *Chill time:* 4 hours

5 cucumbers, peeled, halved, and seeded

1 ½ teaspoons kosher salt, divided

½ cup chopped fresh parsley

6 scallions, chopped

2 tablespoons chopped fresh dill

¼ cup freshly squeezed lemon juice (from about 2 small lemons)

1 quart buttermilk

1 pint full-fat vanilla yogurt

1 teaspoon freshly ground black pepper

1. Place the prepared cucumbers on a shallow plate. Sprinkle with ½ teaspoon of the salt and let stand for 30 minutes.

2. Roughly chop the cucumbers and place in a blender. Add the parsley, scallions, fresh dill, lemon juice, buttermilk, and yogurt, and blend on high until very smooth. Season with the remaining salt and the black pepper.

3. Transfer soup to a bowl. Chill, covered, for at least 4 hours before serving.

ACTING LINES NOODLE SOUP

Don't worry if you keep flubbing your acting lines. Callback auditions are stressful, especially when you're up against your friend's cute kid. This noodle—not tomato—soup will be there for you.

Yield: 4 servings • *Prep time:* 5 minutes • *Cook time:* 25–27 minutes

2 tablespoons extra virgin olive oil

1 rib celery, thinly sliced

1 medium carrot, thinly sliced

1 small yellow onion, finely diced

2 cloves garlic, minced

½ teaspoon kosher salt

1 teaspoon freshly ground black pepper

⅓ cup uncooked orzo noodles

4 cups chicken broth

2 tablespoons finely chopped fresh parsley

1 teaspoon freshly squeezed lemon juice

1. To a medium saucepan set over medium heat, add the olive oil. Add the celery, carrot, and onion. Sprinkle with the salt and pepper, and cook until the vegetables are tender, and the onion is translucent, about 8 minutes. Add the garlic and stir to combine, cooking just an additional minute longer (be careful not to burn the garlic).

2. Add the orzo to the saucepan and cook until the pasta just begins to brown and toast, about 2 minutes. Add the chicken broth and bring to a boil, about 7 minutes.

3. Reduce the heat and let the soup simmer for 8 to 10 minutes, or until the noodles are tender.

4. Stir in the fresh parsley and squeeze in the lemon juice just before serving.

ALL-TIME FAVORITE MEATBALL SUB

If your favorite sandwich is a meatball sub, you have something in common with someone we all know. The tomato sauce spooned over the top of the meatballs has a slight sweetness to it, thanks to brown sugar. This is definitely a sub you'd take a bullet for, or at least, a pretend one.

Yield: 4 servings • *Prep time:* 10 minutes • *Cook time:* 15 minutes

For the meatballs:

1 pound ground chuck

salt and pepper, to taste

1 teaspoon Italian seasoning

1 teaspoon cumin

1 teaspoon garlic powder

2 tablespoons unsalted butter, melted

¼ cup Italian breadcrumbs

1 large egg, lightly beaten

For the tomato sauce:

2 tablespoons unsalted butter, divided

¼ cup diced yellow onion (about 1 small onion)

½ tablespoon crushed red pepper flakes

2 cloves garlic, minced

1 (17.6-ounce) carton crushed tomatoes

1½ tablespoons light brown sugar

1 tablespoon Italian seasoning

1 teaspoon cumin

¼ teaspoon ground nutmeg

salt and pepper, to taste

For the subs:

2 tablespoons unsalted butter, softened

4 hoagie rolls, or 1 thick baguette (quartered), sliced open

3–6 slices provolone cheese

TO MAKE THE MEATBALLS:

1. In a medium bowl, combine all the meatball ingredients with your hands, being mindful not to overwork the meat.

2. Shape the meat mixture into small meatballs, about 1½ to 2 inches in diameter. Place on a small baking sheet or large plate and chill in the refrigerator for 30 minutes.

3. In a medium skillet set over medium-high heat, brown the meatballs on one side for 5 to 7 minutes. Turn the meatballs over to brown on the other side, and cook for an additional 3 to 4 minutes. Remove from the heat and set aside.

TO MAKE THE TOMATO SAUCE:

1. In the same medium skillet used to cook the meatballs, melt 1 tablespoon of the butter over medium heat.

2. Add the diced onion and sauté until translucent, 3 to 4 minutes.

3. Add the crushed red pepper flakes and stir. Stir in the minced garlic for just a minute more, being careful not to burn it.

4. Pour in the crushed tomatoes and reduce the heat to medium-low. Add the brown sugar, salt and pepper, Italian seasoning, cumin, and nutmeg, and stir. Then add the meatballs and let simmer for 20 minutes.

5. Remove from the heat, add the remaining tablespoon of butter and stir.

TO COMPLETE THE SUB:

1. Preheat the oven to its broiler setting.

2. Spread the softened butter on each hoagie roll, and toast on a small baking sheet in the oven for just a minute or two.

3. Spoon about ¼ cup of the tomato sauce on one side of each hoagie roll, top with one slice of provolone, then add three or four meatballs on top of the cheese. If desired, finish with a second slice of provolone on top of the meatballs.

4. Return the baking sheet with the assembled subs to the oven or broiler for 3 to 4 minutes, or until the cheese has melted completely. Serve while hot.

THANKSGIVING LEFTOVERS SANDWICH

Relive Thanksgiving the next day with this oh-so-good creation. This sandwich is made from leftover Thanksgiving turkey and an extra slice of gravy-soaked bread right in the middle, making the concoction marvelously moist. A sandwich this good is steal-worthy, though, so make sure you label it with your name!

Yield: 1 serving • *Prep time:* 5 minutes • *Cook time:* 2 minutes

3 slices white bread
4 ounces turkey, thinly sliced

½ cup leftover turkey stuffing
½ cup turkey gravy

1. In a small saucepan set over medium heat, warm the gravy, about 2 minutes.

2. Place one slice of white bread on a small shallow dish. Spoon half of the turkey gravy on top of the bread and let soak completely while you prepare the rest of the sandwich.

3. Place 2 ounces of sliced turkey on a slice of white bread.

4. Top with some of the turkey stuffing, then spoon a little of the turkey gravy on top of the stuffing.

5. Using either your fingers or a spatula, place the gravy-soaked slice of bread on top of the stuffing on the first slice.

6. Place the remaining turkey and stuffing on the gravy-soaked bread, and top the sandwich with the third slice of bread. Serve immediately.

DINNER

STEAKS AND AN EGGPLANT

If you want to prepare a tasty meal that you and your vegetarian friend will both enjoy, this steak and eggplant recipe will help you out. Just don't eat all five steaks yourself, or you might find yourself down with a case of the meat sweats.

Yield: 6 servings • *Prep time:* 10 minutes • *Cook time:* 12 minutes

For the steaks:

5 (1-inch-thick) rib 62
eye or New York strip steaks

2 teaspoons kosher salt

6 tablespoons unsalted butter

3–4 cloves garlic, finely minced

4 sprigs fresh thyme

For the eggplant:

2 tablespoons olive oil, divided

1 large eggplant, peeled and cut into
½-inch-thick slices

salt and pepper, to taste

⅓ cup dry breadcrumbs

2 tablespoons pecorino cheese, grated

TO COOK THE STEAKS:

1. Remove the steaks from the refrigerator about 30 minutes prior to cooking. Place on a small baking sheet and pat dry with a paper towel (this removes extra moisture, which will help with browning). Coat the steaks with the salt.

2. Preheat a large (12-inch) cast-iron skillet over high heat for about 10 minutes.

3. Carefully place three steaks in the skillet and resist moving them until a crust has formed, about 2 minutes. Using tongs, turn the steaks and continue to cook for an additional 3 to 4 minutes.

4. Add the butter, garlic, and fresh thyme to the skillet. Let the butter melt completely, and tilt the skillet (using a pot holder to prevent burning your hand) so the butter pools. Spoon the butter mixture over the steaks to baste.

5. Remove the steaks from the heat and transfer to a dinner plate to rest. Repeat step 4 with the remaining steaks.

6. Let steaks rest for about 5 minutes, and serve warm.

TO MAKE THE EGGPLANT:

1. Brush 1 tablespoon of olive oil over the eggplant slices, and sprinkle with salt and pepper.

2. Place the dry breadcrumbs in a shallow baking dish and stir in the grated pecorino cheese to combine.

3. Dip each eggplant slice into the breadcrumb mixture.

4. Add the remaining tablespoon of olive oil to a large skillet set over medium-high heat.

5. Add the eggplant slices to the skillet, and cook on each side for 5 minutes, or until golden brown.

6. Remove from the heat, sprinkle with additional salt and pepper to taste. Serve warm.

KIDDIE MAC AND CHEESE

Children love this basic mac cheese version with processed cheese. Add hot dogs, another kid favorite, and you'll have a table of youngsters in the clean plate club. And if your boyfriend happens to have a palate that rivals a 6-year-old boy, he'll appreciate this dish too!

Yield: 8 servings • *Prep time:* 12 minutes • *Cook time:* 5 minutes

1 pound short pasta, such as elbow macaroni, penne, or shells

8 hot dogs, sliced in half and then into half-moons

½ cup full-fat milk

8 ounces processed block cheddar cheese, cubed

1 teaspoon kosher salt

1 teaspoon freshly ground black pepper

¼ teaspoon paprika

1. Cook the pasta according to package instructions. Drain and set aside.

2. While the pasta is cooking, heat a small saucepan over medium heat. Add the milk, processed cheese, salt, black pepper, and paprika. Whisk until cheese has melted and mixture is smooth, about 5 minutes.

3. Drain the pasta and return to pot. Pour the cheese sauce over the pasta, then stir in the hot dogs.

4. Let macaroni and cheese cool slightly before serving.

THANKSGIVING TURKEY FOR ONE

The juiciest, tastiest Thanksgiving turkey you can have, should you choose to do individual protein dishes one year. This recipe makes enough turkey for two servings, so you can still have those day-after leftovers. We recommend putting on your eating pants before conquering this mountain.

Yield: 2 servings • *Prep time:* 10 minutes • *Cook time:* 45–55 minutes

1 skin-on, bone-in turkey breast
6 tablespoons unsalted butter, softened
2 teaspoons kosher salt
2 teaspoons freshly ground black pepper

3 sprigs fresh thyme
2 sprigs fresh rosemary
½ head garlic, cloves peeled and crushed

1. Preheat the oven to 425°F.

2. Using your hands, gently loosen the skin on the turkey breast and rub butter under the skin and over the entire breast. Season with the salt and black pepper.

3. Place the thyme and rosemary sprigs and crushed garlic cloves on a large rimmed baking sheet, and place the turkey breast on top, skin side up.

4. Roast the turkey breast, turning the whole baking sheet halfway through the baking time to ensure even browning, for 45 to 55 minutes, or until the skin is crispy and the thickest part of the turkey breast registers 160°F on an instant-read thermometer.

5. Transfer to a platter and let rest for 15 minutes before carving and serving.

CHICKEN POX SPAGHETTI AND SALAD

In case your friend and her military boyfriend come down with a case of chicken pox, this spaghetti and salad recipe can be a nice way to take care of (spy on) them.

Yield: 2 to 4 servings • *Prep time:* 10 minutes • *Cook time:* 30 minutes

For the spaghetti:

1 (8-ounce) package spaghetti

1 tablespoon unsalted butter

1 pound ground turkey

1 teaspoon kosher salt

1 teaspoon freshly ground black pepper

1 teaspoon ground cumin

1 teaspoon Italian seasoning

1 teaspoon cayenne

1 (15-ounce) can tomato sauce

For the salad:

½ head romaine lettuce, torn into ½-inch pieces

½ small cucumber, peeled, seeded, and diced

½ Roma tomato, seeded and quartered

2–4 tablespoons store-bought Italian dressing, or to taste

¼ teaspoon kosher salt

¼ teaspoon freshly cracked black pepper

TO MAKE THE SPAGHETTI:

1. Cook the spaghetti according to package instructions. Drain pasta and let cool.

2. While the spaghetti is cooking, start the turkey tomato sauce. In a medium skillet set over medium heat, melt the butter. Add the ground turkey, salt, black pepper, ground cumin, Italian seasoning, and cayenne. Cook until the meat browns, 5 to 7 minutes.

3. Add the tomato sauce, turn the heat to medium-high, and bring to a gentle boil. Reduce the heat to low and let simmer for an additional 10 minutes.

4. Add the turkey tomato mixture to the pasta pot and toss with tongs. Let cool slightly while you make the salad.

TO MAKE THE SALAD:

1. In a medium mixing bowl, toss together the romaine lettuce, cucumber, and tomato with tongs.

2. When you're ready to serve, drizzle dressing on the salad and season with salt and black pepper. Toss again with tongs. Serve immediately with the spaghetti.

TURKEY BURGERS

You can make this delicious turkey burger on the stove for a quick weekday meal or on the grill at a fight-night apartment-balcony cookout. Could this *be* any more perfect?

Yield: 4 servings • *Prep time:* 5 minutes • *Cook time:* 10 minutes • *Chill time:* 10 minutes

1 pound ground turkey

1 large egg, lightly beaten

1 teaspoon kosher salt

1 teaspoon freshly ground black pepper

1 teaspoon cumin

1 teaspoon garlic powder

3 tablespoons unsalted butter, melted

1. In a medium bowl, combine the ground turkey, beaten egg, salt, black pepper, cumin, garlic powder, and melted butter with your hands or a wooden spoon. Shape the mixture into four 1-inch-thick patties. Place the patties on a small baking sheet or dinner plate, cover with plastic wrap, and chill in the refrigerator for 10 minutes or up to overnight. (Patties can be made 1 day ahead.)

2. Spray a large (12-inch) cast-iron skillet with cooking spray and set over medium heat.

3. Add the patties to the skillet and cook on one side for 5 minutes, or until the patties begin to brown. Flip the patties and cook for an additional 5 minutes, or until golden brown.

4. Serve on hamburger buns with toppings of your choice.

POLITICAL COMMENTATOR MUSHROOM, GREEN PEPPER, AND ONION PIZZA

A great vegetarian pizza for you, your bestie, or maybe your famous political commentator neighbor across the way? This is a great meal to have with the Tiki Death Punch on page 148. Use the leftover vegetable mixture as the filling for a delicious vegetable-packed quiche.

Yield: 6 servings • *Prep time:* 5 minutes • *Cook time:* 15 minutes

1 (12-inch) store-bought pizza crust
1 tablespoon unsalted butter
1 small yellow onion, sliced into strips
1 small green pepper, sliced into strips

⅓ cup button mushrooms, sliced (about 4 to 5 mushrooms)
½ teaspoon crushed red pepper flakes
1½–2 cups store-bought tomato sauce
8 ounces mozzarella cheese, grated

1. Preheat the oven according to directions on the pizza crust package.

2. In a medium skillet set over medium heat, melt the butter. Add the sliced onion and sauté until it becomes translucent, 3 to 4 minutes. Add the green pepper strips and continue to sauté until tender, an additional 4 to 5 minutes. Add the sliced mushrooms and sauté for a minute or two more, or until just slightly tender. Be mindful not to overcook the mushrooms. Sprinkle in the crushed red pepper flakes and stir to incorporate. Remove the vegetable mixture from the heat.

3. Place the pizza crust on a large baking sheet. Spoon about half of the tomato sauce in the center of the crust. Using the ladle, spread the sauce in a circular motion to cover the entire pizza, leaving about an inch of the edge of the crust uncovered. Spoon the remaining half of sauce in the center of the pizza and spread it.

4. Sprinkle about half of the shredded mozzarella over the pizza, then spoon the vegetable mixture on top of the cheese. Add more cheese on top of the vegetable mixture if you like.

5. Bake for 7 to 8 minutes, or follow the directions on the pizza crust package.

FUNERAL RECEPTION HONEY-GLAZED HAM

This sweet ham is good for all occasions: Easter, Christmas, or even a funeral reception. And if your grandmother happens to have died twice, this is exactly the ham she'd want.

Yield: 12 to 14 servings • *Prep time:* 20 minutes • *Cook time:* 2 hours

3 tablespoons unsalted butter

2 tablespoons chopped fresh oregano

1 (12–14 pound) boneless fully cooked ham

¼ cup apple cider vinegar

½ cup honey

1 teaspoon Worcestershire sauce

1. In a small saucepan set over medium heat, melt the butter with the chopped oregano. Set aside.

2. Preheat the oven to 350°F.

3. Peel off and discard any rind from the ham, leaving a ¼-inch or so layer of fat. Score the fat in a crosshatch pattern, making sure not to cut into the meat.

4. Transfer the ham to a rack placed in a large roasting pan. Cover the ham with parchment paper, then cover the roasting pan with aluminum foil. Bake for 1 hour.

5. In a small saucepan set over medium-high heat, reduce the vinegar to about 1 tablespoon. Remove from the heat and whisk in the honey, Worcestershire sauce, and the reserved oregano butter. Set aside while the ham bakes.

6. After the ham has baked for an hour, remove and discard the parchment and aluminum foil. If all the liquid in the roasting pan has evaporated, add 1 cup of water to the pan. Then, using a pastry brush, brush the ham with half of the honey mixture. Bake, uncovered, for an additional 30 minutes.

7. After the 30 minutes, brush on the remaining glaze and bake for a final 30 minutes, or until the glaze is deep golden brown.

8. Remove from the oven, transfer to a platter, and let rest for 15 minutes before slicing.

TV DINNER PIGS IN A BLANKET

This recipe takes the classic pigs in a blanket hors d'oeuvres—that would make a lovely menu option for a wedding with two brides—and turns it into a great dinner for watching your favorite television show.

Yield: 8 servings • *Prep time:* 10 minutes • *Cook time:* 14 minutes

8 hot dogs, slit about halfway down and within ½ inch of ends

4 ounces mild cheddar cheese, sliced into thin strips

1 (8-ounce) can refrigerated crescent rolls

1. Preheat the oven to 375°F. Line one large baking sheet with parchment paper.

2. Insert one or two strips of the cheddar cheese into each hot dog.

3. Unfurl the crescent rolls and separate into triangles. Wrap a crescent roll around each hot dog, cheese side up. Place on the prepared baking sheet.

4. Bake for 14 minutes, or until the crescent rolls are golden brown (darkest around the edges) and the cheese has melted.

5. Serve hot.

GRILLED CHEESE AND ALL THAT

Your first Friendsgiving pretty much means things might not always go as planned. So if you find you've burnt the turkey and stuffing, there's always grilled cheese to fill your tummy. Throw in some Funyuns and a bottle of wine and you got yourself a party. The best part is, there's no chance of a grilled cheese getting stuck on anyone's head—no matter how hard you try.

Yield: 4 servings • *Prep time:* 10 minutes • *Cook time:* 20 minutes

8 slices white sandwich bread
½ cup unsalted butter, divided

8 slices cheddar cheese
1 (6-ounce) bag Funyuns

1. Spread about 1 tablespoon of butter on each of slice of bread. Set aside.

2. Place two slices of bread buttered side down in a large skillet set over medium heat. Top with two slices of cheddar cheese. Place a buttered side up slice of bread on top of the cheddar and cook until the cheese just begins to melt and the bread has browned slightly, about 5 minutes. Using a large spatula, flip each grilled cheese and cook for an additional 2 to 3 minutes, or until the cheese has melted completely and the bread is toasted and golden brown.

3. Repeat with the remaining slices of bread and cheese.

4. Serve grilled cheeses on a platter with Funyuns with a 750-milliliter bottle of white wine.

TWO CHICKS CHICKEN BREASTS

In case the wedding caterer gets in a mountain bike accident, this recipe for two chicken breasts sautéed in a skillet and finished off in the oven is more than good enough in a pinch. It's perfect on the menu for one New York City lesbian couple's wedding. Or is that too cute?

Yield: 2 servings • *Prep time:* 5 minutes • *Cook time:* 25 minutes

2 large skinless chicken breasts

1 teaspoon kosher salt

1 teaspoon freshly ground black pepper

1 teaspoon garlic powder

2 tablespoons extra virgin olive oil, divided

zest and juice from 1 small lemon

½ teaspoon fresh thyme, chopped

1. Preheat the oven to 350°F.

2. Place the chicken breasts on a dinner plate or a plastic cutting board, and season with the salt, pepper, and garlic powder. Line a small baking sheet with aluminum foil.

3. In a large skillet set over medium heat, drizzle 1 tablespoon of olive oil. Add both chicken breasts and cook on one side for 5 minutes. Add the lemon zest and lemon juice to both chicken breasts. Resist moving or turning the chicken for the first 5 minutes. Turn the chicken breasts and cook on the other side for an additional 5 minutes. Transfer to the prepared baking sheet and sprinkle the thyme on top of each chicken breast.

4. Bake the chicken breasts for 15 minutes. Serve hot.

JEWELRY BOX MAC AND CHEESE

This flavorful mac and cheese is a real party pleaser. Just don't get your pasta off a macaroni jewelry box. That's just gross, even if you are stuck in your room with no dinner.

Yield: 8 servings • *Prep time:* 5 to 7 minutes • *Cook time:* 45 minutes

1 pound short pasta, such as elbow macaroni, penne, or shells

2 tablespoons unsalted butter

¼ cup finely diced shallots (about 2 small shallots)

2 cloves garlic, finely minced

3 tablespoons all-purpose flour

2 cups whole milk

½ cup heavy cream

1½ cup shredded cheddar cheese

1½ cup shredded Havarti cheese

½ cup freshly grated Parmesan cheese, divided

1 teaspoon salt, or to taste

1 teaspoon black pepper, or to taste

1 teaspoon cumin

1 teaspoon dried oregano

1 cup Italian breadcrumbs

1. Preheat the oven to 400°F.

2. Cook the pasta according to package instructions. Drain and set aside.

3. In a large saucepan over medium heat, melt the butter. Add the shallots and garlic, stirring frequently to avoid burning the garlic. Cook until the shallots are translucent, 3 to 4 minutes.

4. Sprinkle the flour into the saucepan. Stir constantly with a wooden spoon until the flour has been fully incorporated into the shallots and garlic, about 1 to 2 minutes.

5. Slowly pour in the milk and heavy cream, and whisk to combine. Bring to a boil, then reduce the heat to medium-low.

6. Whisk in all of the shredded cheddar and Havarti cheeses, along with ¼ cup of the Parmesan cheese. Whisk in the salt, black pepper, cumin, and dried oregano to combine. Continue to whisk until the cheeses have melted. Remove from the heat.

7. Pour the cheese sauce over the cooled pasta, and stir to combine. Transfer to a 9 x 13-inch casserole dish. Sprinkle the breadcrumbs and the remaining Parmesan cheese over the mixture.

8. Bake for 30 minutes, or until the top has browned nicely and the cheese sauce is bubbling.

9. Let cool slightly before serving.

CALIFORNIA ROLL

A nice California sushi roll for when you'd like to re-create the sushi you had on a Manhattan dinner date. You'll need a sushi mat for this recipe. You can find one easily on the internet or at World Market stores. Sushi making is a delicate art, so make sure you're in a state of total awareness before prepping this dish.

Yield: 6 servings • *Prep time:* 5 minutes • *Cook time:* 20 minutes

2 cups uncooked sushi rice, rinsed and drained

2 cups water

¼ cup rice wine vinegar

2 tablespoons granulated sugar

½ teaspoon kosher salt

2 tablespoons sesame seeds, toasted

8 nori sheets

1 small cucumber, seeded and cut into thin strips

3 ounces crab meat, cut into thin strips

1 medium ripe avocado, cut into thin strips

soy sauce, prepared wasabi, and pickled ginger, to serve

1. In a large saucepan, combine the rice and water. Let stand for 30 minutes. Bring to a boil over medium-high, then reduce the heat to low and simmer for 15 to 20 minutes. Remove from the heat and let stand until the rice has cooled, 10 to 15 minutes.

2. In a small bowl, whisk the rice wine vinegar, sugar, and salt until sugar and salt are dissolved.

3. On a large baking sheet, spread the rice into a single layer with a wooden spatula. Drizzle the vinegar mixture over the rice and stir. Cover with a damp kitchen towel.

4. Sprinkle sesame seeds on a plate and set aside.

5. Line a sushi mat with plastic wrap. Spoon about ¾ cup sushi rice on the mat. Press the rice into an 8-inch square. Top the rice with one sheet of nori.

6. Arrange the cucumber, crab meat, and avocado slices on top of the nori, stopping about ½ inch from the edge of the nori sheet.

7. Using the sushi mat, tightly roll the sushi into a log. Remove the plastic wrap as you roll.

8. Roll the sushi log in the reserved sesame seeds, then wrap in plastic wrap and chill in the refrigerator as you make another sushi log.

9. Repeat steps 5 to 8 with the remaining rice, cucumber, crab meat, and avocado. Slice each sushi log into eight pieces.

10. Serve the sushi rolls with soy sauce, prepared wasabi, and pickled ginger.

SPECIAL PIZZAS

This "special" is really just two pepperoni pies, which is about as perfect a pizza order as one can imagine. These pies might also be paired with a beer as a "thank you" to your friends for helping you move. As we all know, it is no easy feat getting furniture up a tiny stairwell. They deserve a slice after all that pivoting!

Yield: 16 servings • *Prep time:* 9 minutes • *Cook time:* 16 minutes

2 (12-inch) ready-made pizza crusts

1 (17.6-ounce) carton crushed tomatoes

2 tablespoons light brown sugar

1 teaspoon kosher salt

1 teaspoon freshly ground black pepper

1 teaspoon ground cumin

1 teaspoon Italian seasoning

10 ounces mozzarella cheese, grated

10 ounces sliced pepperoni

1. Preheat the oven to 450°F. Line two large unrimmed baking sheets with aluminum foil and spray with cooking spray. Place the pizza crusts on the prepared baking sheets.

2. To a small saucepan set over medium heat, add the crushed tomatoes, brown sugar, salt, black pepper, cumin, and Italian seasoning. Stir to incorporate and cook just until the tomato sauce has warmed through, 5 to 7 minutes. Remove from the heat.

3. Spoon one ladleful of the sauce in the center of one of the pizza crusts. Use the ladle to spread the sauce evenly on the crust, leaving a 1-inch border. Sprinkle about a third of the mozzarella cheese over the sauce, then top with half of the pepperoni. Sprinkle a bit more cheese on top.

4. Repeat with the second pizza crust.

5. Bake the pizzas one at a time for 8 to 10 minutes or until the crust becomes golden brown and the cheese is bubbly.

BETTER THAN TAKEOUT FRIED CHICKEN

An excellent fried chicken recipe to make at home, one that will surpass the kind that you take home in a red and white bucket. This chicken will come out golden and crispy, but we recommend eating the whole thing, not just the skin. And don't worry—your friend's fowl roommates were NOT harmed in the making of this recipe!

Yield: 4 servings • *Prep time:* 10 minutes • *Cook time:* 24 minutes • *Chill time:* 8 hours

2 tablespoons kosher salt, divided

2 teaspoons freshly ground black pepper

¾ teaspoon cayenne pepper

½ teaspoon garlic powder

4 bone-in, skin-on chicken thighs

1 cup buttermilk

1 large egg

2 tablespoons hot sauce

2 cups all-purpose flour

1 tablespoon cornstarch

canola oil, for frying

1. In a small mixing bowl, whisk together 1 tablespoon of the salt with the black pepper, cayenne pepper, and garlic powder. Place the chicken thighs on a dinner plate and season with the spices. Cover with plastic wrap and chill overnight.

2. Let the chicken stand covered at room temperature for 1 hour.

3. Whisk the buttermilk, egg, and hot sauce in a shallow dish, and set aside. In another shallow dish, whisk together the flour, cornstarch and remaining tablespoon of salt.

4. Pour enough oil into a 12-inch cast-iron skillet so it's about 2 inches deep. Place a fry thermometer into the oil and bring to 350°F over medium-high heat.

5. Meanwhile, place a wire cooling rack in a large rimmed baking sheet. Dip one chicken piece at a time into the buttermilk mixture making sure to shake off excess liquid. Place the same chicken piece in the dish with the flour mixture. Coat well, shaking off any excess. Place the dredged chicken piece back onto the dinner plate. Repeat with the remaining chicken pieces.

6. Place all four pieces of chicken into the hot oil, turning frequently with tongs to ensure even frying. Cook about 12 minutes, or until golden brown and a meat thermometer registers 165°F.

7. Remove the fried chicken from the oil and place on the cooling rack in the baking sheet. Sprinkle a bit of salt on each piece immediately. Let cool slightly before serving.

ENGAGEMENT RING LASAGNA

You'll find no ring in this lasagna recipe (engagement or otherwise), just lots of cheese and layers stacked to high heaven.

Yield: 9 servings • *Prep time:* 60 minutes • *Cook time:* 40 to 45 minutes

1 (16-ounce) package dry lasagna noodles (not "no-boil")

1 tablespoon unsalted butter

1 tablespoon olive oil

¼ cup finely diced shallots (about 2 small shallots)

3 cloves garlic, finely diced

1 tablespoon tomato paste

1 pound ground sweet Italian sausage

1½ teaspoons garlic powder

1½ teaspoons Italian seasoning

1½ teaspoons cumin

2 (17.6-ounce) cartons crushed tomatoes

1 tablespoon brown sugar

24 ounces mozzarella cheese, grated

8 ounces Parmesan cheese, grated

fresh parsley, roughly chopped

salt and pepper, to taste

1. Preheat the oven to 400°F.

2. Cook the lasagna noodles according to package directions. Lay lasagna noodles on kitchen towels to dry separately.

3. In a medium sauté pan set over medium heat, melt the butter with the olive oil. Add the shallots and sauté until barely translucent, 1 to 2 minutes. Add the garlic and continue to cook, about 2 minutes more, keeping an eye on the garlic to make sure it doesn't burn. Add the tomato paste and stir to incorporate with the shallots and garlic.

4. Add the ground Italian sausage and break up with a wooden spoon to ensure even cooking.

5. Add the garlic powder, Italian seasoning, cumin, and salt and pepper, and stir. Cook until the sausage has browned, about 7 minutes.

6. Pour in the crushed tomatoes, and add the brown sugar as well as more salt and pepper to taste. Stir and let simmer on low anywhere from 15 minutes to an hour.

7. Spoon about ¼ cup of the sauce onto the bottom of a 9 x 13-inch casserole dish.

8. Arrange three noodles in a single layer. Sprinkle a handful of the mozzarella and Parmesan cheeses, top with more sauce, and sprinkle another handful of the cheeses. Repeat this step three more times.

9. Once the lasagna has been assembled, cover loosely with aluminum foil and bake for 20 minutes.

10. After 20 minutes, remove the foil and continue to bake for an additional 20 to 25 minutes, or until the lasagna begins to bubble. Sprinkle with chopped fresh parsley immediately after removing from the oven.

11. Let the lasagna cool for at least 30 minutes (longer, if you have the time) before cutting into it and serving.

GROUND BEEF TACOS

If you know you will be riding a roller coaster later, maybe refrain from eating these tacos beforehand. These are delicious, but eating ten of them could make you feel just a little bit iffy.

Yield: 5 to 10 servings • *Prep time:* 10 minutes • *Cook time:* 20–25 minutes

2 tablespoons canola oil

1 small yellow onion, diced (about ¼ cup)

1 pound ground chuck

3 cloves garlic, finely diced

1 teaspoon kosher salt

1 teaspoon freshly ground black pepper

1 teaspoon ground cumin

1 teaspoon chili powder

10 ready-made hard taco shells

Toppings:

8 ounces Colby Jack cheese, grated

sour cream

avocado slices

hot sauce

1. Preheat the oven to 330°F.

2. Line a large baking sheet with aluminum foil and set aside.

3. In a large skillet set over medium heat, drizzle in the canola oil and add the diced onion. Cook until translucent, 3 to 4 minutes.

4. Add the ground chuck, garlic, salt, black pepper, cumin, and chili powder. Cook, stirring frequently, until the ground chuck has browned completely, about 7 to 10 minutes. Remove from the heat.

5. Place the taco shells on the prepared baking sheet and warm in the oven for 7 minutes.

6. Using a small slotted spoon, fill each taco shell with the meat mixture. Add preferred toppings and serve immediately.

SPICY ENCHILADAS

These enchiladas are so spicy (and delicious) they might even induce labor. Yes, they really are that good!

Yield: 6 to 8 servings • *Prep time:* 8 minutes • *Cook time:* 45 minutes

1 tablespoon unsalted butter

1 small yellow onion, finely diced

1 pound ground chuck

1 teaspoon kosher salt

1 teaspoon freshly ground black pepper

1 teaspoon ground cumin

1 heaping tablespoon chili powder

1 chipotle pepper, finely diced

3 cloves garlic, finely minced

2 (10-ounce) cans spicy enchilada sauce

¼ cup canola oil, for frying

12 (6-inch) corn tortillas

16 ounces Monterey Jack cheese, grated

1. Line a small plate with paper towels and set aside.

2. To a medium skillet set over medium heat, add the butter and diced onion. Cook until translucent, 3 to 4 minutes.

3. Add the ground chuck, salt, black pepper, ground cumin, chili powder, and chipotle pepper to the skillet. Cook until the meat has browned, 5 to 7 minutes. Add the garlic, stir, and cook just until the garlic is fragrant, 1 to 2 minutes. Remove the meat mixture from the heat and set aside.

4. To a small saucepan set over low heat, add both cans of enchilada sauce and heat just until warmed, 3 to 4 minutes, then turn off the heat.

5. Preheat the oven to 375°F.

6. To a small skillet set over medium-high heat, add the canola oil and let it heat for 5 minutes. Using tongs, carefully and slowly drop one corn tortilla at a time into the oil and allow to fry for 1 minute on each side. The goal is to cook the tortilla just enough to make it easier to roll. The added benefit is that a lightly fried tortilla has a great bite and chew.

7. After lightly frying the tortilla, place it on the prepared paper towel-lined plate to drain the oil, just for a second each. Drop the tortilla into the saucepan with the enchilada sauce. Using tongs, turn the tortilla over carefully to coat with the sauce. Transfer the coated tortilla to a dinner plate and repeat with the remaining tortillas.

8. Spoon one ladleful of enchilada sauce evenly on the bottom of a 9 x 13-inch baking dish.

9. Spoon about 2 tablespoons of meat mixture onto a tortilla, then sprinkle about 1 tablespoon of grated Monterey Jack on top. Carefully roll the tortilla up over itself to make an enchilada. Place the enchilada seam-side down in the baking dish. Repeat with the remaining tortillas.

10. Spoon about half of the remaining enchilada sauce over the enchiladas and sprinkle with the remaining cheese. (The remaining enchilada sauce can be transferred to an air-tight container and kept in the refrigerator for up to a week. Spoon leftover enchilada sauce over scrambled eggs, or as a condiment on Mexican-inspired burgers.)

11. Bake for 25 minutes, or until the cheese is bubbling and the enchiladas are warmed through. Serve immediately.

BIRTHDAY PARTY HAMBURGERS AND COLESLAW

A simple but delicious and juicy hamburger with a side of slaw to make for a best friend's birthday party. Even if her presents are disappointing, this burger will save the day.

Yield: 6 servings • *Prep time:* 10 minutes • *Cook time:* 25 minutes

For the hamburgers:

2 pounds ground chuck

1 tablespoon onion powder

1 teaspoon seasoned salt

1 teaspoon kosher salt

1 teaspoon freshly ground black pepper

6 hamburger buns

6 slices cheddar cheese (optional)

For the coleslaw:

1 cup mayonnaise

1 ½ tablespoon apple cider vinegar

1 tablespoon honey

1 teaspoon kosher salt

½ teaspoon freshly ground black pepper

½ medium green cabbage, thinly sliced

½ medium red cabbage, thinly sliced

2 medium carrots, grated

TO MAKE THE HAMBURGERS:

1. In a large mixing bowl, combine the ground chuck, onion powder, seasoned salt, kosher salt, and black pepper using your hands or a wooden spoon. Be mindful not to overmix the meat.

2. Divide the mixture into six patties. Preheat a 10-inch cast-iron skillet on high heat and add the patties (three at a time to avoid overcrowding the skillet).

3. Cook the patties until a crust forms, 2 to 3 minutes. Gently flip the burgers using a spatula. If using, place a slice of cheese on top of each patty. Continue to cook for 2 to 3 minutes for rare or medium rare; 4 to 5 minutes for more well done.

4. Remove from the heat, place on the buns, and serve with your preferred toppings.

TO MAKE THE COLESLAW:

1. In a large bowl, whisk together the mayonnaise, apple cider vinegar, honey, salt, and black pepper. Add both cabbages and the grated carrots, and toss to coat.

2. Cover the bowl with plastic wrap and chill in the refrigerator at least 1 hour, or up to 8 hours.

TOP-NOTCH TOMATO SAUCE

This tomato sauce is slightly sweet, thanks to a couple of tablespoons of brown sugar, which combats the acidity in the tomatoes. Everyone will love the sauce whether they're food critics or not. Who knows, it might even help you land your dream job!

Yield: 3 cups • *Prep time:* 5 minutes • *Cook time:* 25 minutes

2 tablespoons unsalted butter, divided

¼ cup diced yellow onion (about 1 small onion)

½ tablespoon crushed red pepper flakes

2 cloves garlic, minced

1 (17.6-ounce) carton crushed tomatoes

1 ½ tablespoons light brown sugar

1 tablespoon Italian seasoning

1 teaspoon cumin

¼ teaspoon ground nutmeg

salt and pepper, to taste

1. In a medium saucepan set over medium heat, melt 1 tablespoon of the butter.

2. Add the diced onion and sauté until translucent, 3 to 4 minutes.

3. Add the crushed red pepper flakes and stir. Stir in the minced garlic for just a minute more, being careful not to burn it.

4. Pour in the crushed tomatoes and reduce the heat to medium-low. Add the brown sugar, salt and pepper, Italian seasoning, cumin, and nutmeg, and stir. Let the sauce simmer over medium-low heat for 20 minutes.

5. Remove from the heat, add the remaining tablespoon of butter, and stir.

6. You may serve tomato sauce immediately over your favorite pasta, for example, or chill sauce for up to 2 days in your refrigerator.

CRITICAL PARENTS SPAGHETTI

Should your parents show up at your New York City apartment, have you got a delicious spaghetti to serve them? Well, now you do. This recipe is...easy. But in a good way!

Yield: 6 servings • *Prep time:* 5 minutes • *Cook time:* 25 minutes

1 (16-ounce) package spaghetti

2 tablespoons unsalted butter, divided

¼ cup diced yellow onion (about 1 small onion)

½ tablespoon crushed red pepper flakes

1 pound ground sweet Italian sausage

2 cloves garlic, minced

1 (17.6-ounce) carton crushed tomatoes

1½ tablespoons light brown sugar

1 tablespoon Italian seasoning

1 teaspoon garlic powder

1 teaspoon cumin

¼ teaspoon ground nutmeg

Parmesan cheese, grated (optional)

salt and pepper, to taste

1. Cook the spaghetti according to package instructions. Drain and set aside.

2. In a medium skillet set over medium heat, melt 1 tablespoon of butter. Add the diced onion and crushed red pepper flakes, and sauté until the onion becomes translucent, 3 to 4 minutes.

3. Add the sausage and continue to sauté until browned, 5 to 6 minutes.

4. Add the garlic and stir, being careful not to burn it (reduce the heat to low, if needed).

5. Pour in the crushed tomatoes. Add the brown sugar, salt and pepper, Italian seasoning, garlic powder, cumin, and ground nutmeg, and stir.

6. Reduce the heat to low (if you didn't when adding the garlic), and let the sauce simmer for 15 minutes. Remove from the heat, add the remaining tablespoon of butter, and stir to incorporate.

7. Add the drained and cooled spaghetti, and toss with tongs to coat completely with the sauce.

8. Use the tongs to serve. Sprinkle Parmesan cheese on top of each serving, if desired.

SCANDALOUS MOM KUNG PAO CHICKEN

Eat this spicy kung pao chicken as you watch your feisty, flirtatious mom be a guest on a late-night television talk show. It is so good, it might even help you get over any lingering issues from your childhood.

Yield: 4 servings • *Prep time:* 40 minutes • *Cook time:* 5 to 6 minutes

1 tablespoon cornstarch

4 tablespoons soy sauce

1 pound boneless, skinless chicken breasts, cut into ½-inch pieces

3 tablespoons rice wine vinegar

2 tablespoons granulated sugar

3 tablespoons chicken stock

4 teaspoons balsamic vinegar

1 tablespoon sesame oil

3 tablespoons peanut oil

6 dried hot chiles, seeded and thinly sliced

5 scallions, thinly sliced, divided

3 cloves garlic, finely minced

1 tablespoon finely minced fresh ginger

⅓ cup roughly chopped peanuts

1. In a small mixing bowl, whisk the cornstarch and soy sauce to combine. Add the chicken and toss to coat. Let marinate in the refrigerator for 30 minutes.

2. In another small mixing bowl, whisk the rice wine vinegar, sugar, chicken stock, balsamic vinegar, and sesame oil to combine. Set aside.

3. Set a large nonstick skillet or wok over high heat and add the peanut oil. When the oil begins to smoke, add the marinated chicken, the hot chiles, half of the scallions, and the garlic and fresh ginger. Stir and toss constantly to ensure even cooking. Cook until the chicken is golden brown, 5 to 6 minutes.

4. Stir in the peanuts and scallions, then transfer to a serving platter. Serve hot.

SIZZLING FAJITAS

Even if you are drunk and distracted, please try to remember to wear oven mitts while carrying a sizzling-hot pan of fajitas to the table. You'll thank me in the morning.

Yield: 4 servings • *Prep time:* 10 minutes • *Cook time:* 15–20 minutes

1 tablespoon canola oil

1 pound flank steak, sliced thinly

1½ teaspoons kosher salt, divided

2 teaspoons freshly ground black pepper, divided

1 teaspoon ground cumin

1 teaspoon chili powder

1 tablespoon unsalted butter

1 small yellow onion, sliced into half-moons

1 medium orange bell pepper, sliced into half-moons

2 cloves garlic, finely minced

8 (6-inch) corn tortillas

1. In a small skillet set over medium heat, drizzle the canola oil. Let the oil heat for just a minute or two, then add the sliced flank steak. Season with 1 teaspoon of the salt, 1 teaspoon of the black pepper, and the ground cumin and chili powder. Cook until the steak has browned, 5 to 7 minutes. Remove from the skillet and transfer to a small bowl. Leave the skillet set over medium heat.

2. To the skillet, add the butter. Once the butter has melted, add the sliced onion and cook until just slightly translucent, 2 to 3 minutes. Add the bell pepper and garlic, and season with the remaining salt and pepper. Cook until the bell pepper is tender, about 5 minutes. Remove from the heat.

3. Return the steak to the skillet and toss to incorporate with the vegetables.

4. Heat the tortillas over low heat on your stove. Use tongs to flip the tortillas.

5. Place two tortillas on each plate and scoop steak and vegetable mixture onto each. Serve hot.

BREAKUP PIZZA

If you're going through a break up, or are in the midst of a blowout fight, a pizza can be just what you need. You might think anchovy pizza is not your thing, but give this one a try. There aren't any cut up anchovies in the sauce, so if you really need to pick around them, you still can. It won't solve all your relationship problems, but at least you'll be well fed.

Yield: 6 servings • *Prep time:* 10 minutes • *Cook time:* 8 to 10 minutes

1 (12-inch) ready-made pizza crust
½ cup canned tomato sauce
15 anchovy fillets

8 ounces mozzarella cheese, grated
2 heaping teaspoons capers
1 tablespoon Italian seasoning

1. Preheat the oven to 450°F.

2. Place the pizza crust on a large ungreased baking sheet. Spoon the tomato sauce in the center of the crust. With a ladle, spread the sauce evenly over the crust, leaving a 1-inch border around the edge.

3. Place the anchovy fillets over the pizza, then top with the mozzarella cheese. Add the capers and Italian seasoning. Bake for 8 to 10 minutes, or until the crust is golden brown and the cheese has melted.

PONZU GINGER SHRIMP RAVIOLI

If as part of a job interview, you need to provide your "high on life" potential boss with something for his munchies, this classic shrimp ravioli will keep him happy. This recipe makes four servings, but you'll probably want to eat a hundred of them. If you don't keep ponzu sauce on hand, feel free to substitute with ¼ cup rice wine vinegar, 1 tablespoon lime juice (from about 1 small lime), and 1 tablespoon bottled orange juice.

Yield: 4 servings • *Prep time:* 10 minutes • *Cook time:* 10 minutes

1 (10-ounce) package spinach ravioli

1 tablespoon unsalted butter

¼ cup finely minced shallot (about 2 small shallots)

1 pound frozen, uncooked rock shrimp

¼ teaspoon kosher salt

1 teaspoon freshly cracked black pepper

1 teaspoon paprika

2 cloves garlic, finely minced

1 tablespoon fresh ginger, finely minced

1 cup teriyaki sauce

⅓ cup ponzu sauce

½ teaspoon red pepper flakes

1 tablespoon fresh cilantro, roughly chopped

1. Cook the ravioli according to package instructions. Let cool as you cook the shrimp.

2. In a medium skillet set over medium heat, melt the butter. Add the shallot and cook until just barely translucent, 2 to 3 minutes. Add the shrimp, salt, black pepper, and paprika. Lower the heat to medium-low and add the garlic, stirring to incorporate. Cook the shrimp for about 3 minutes on each side, or until no longer pink. Be careful to not overcook them.

3. Transfer the shrimp to a small plate. Add the teriyaki sauce; the ponzu sauce or the ¼ cup rice wine vinegar, teaspoon of lime juice, and tablespoon of orange juice; and the red pepper flakes to the same skillet. Turn the heat to medium-high and whisk to fully combine. Cook just until sauce begins to boil gently, about 2 minutes. Whisk in the chopped cilantro and remove from heat.

4. Spoon the ravioli onto a large platter or into a large serving bowl. Pour the sauce over the ravioli and toss gently just to combine. Top with the shrimp and serve immediately.

STEAK FRIED RICE

A great steak fried rice to eat while sitting around your living room chatting with friends. Best to eat with a fork and save your chopsticks—you never know when you might need them to fashion some sort of poking device.

Yield: 4 servings • *Prep time:* 35 to 40 minutes • *Cook time:* 35 minutes

2 cups beef stock

1 cup uncooked short-grain rice

1 tablespoon extra virgin olive oil

1 pound bottom round steak, cut into 1-inch pieces

1 teaspoon kosher salt

1 teaspoon freshly cracked black pepper

1 teaspoon cayenne

1 tablespoon plum sauce

¼ cup diced yellow onion

2 large carrots, sliced into half-moons

⅓ cup frozen peas

2 cloves garlic, finely diced

½ tablespoon unsalted butter

2 large eggs

2 tablespoons soy sauce

2 tablespoons roughly chopped fresh cilantro

1. To a small saucepan set over medium-high heat, add the beef stock. Bring to a boil, then add the rice. Reduce the heat to medium-low, cover the pot, and simmer until the rice is tender, about 20 minutes. Remove from the heat and let cool.

2. To a large skillet set over medium heat, add the olive oil. Once the oil just barely begins to smoke, add the steak. Season with the salt, black pepper, and cayenne. Cook for 3 to 4 minutes, then add the plum sauce. Cook just an additional minute, then transfer to a small bowl.

3. In the same skillet used to cook the steak, add the diced onion. Cook just until barely translucent, 2 to 3 minutes, then add the sliced carrots. Cook until the carrots are tender, about 5 minutes. Add the frozen peas and garlic. Stir to incorporate.

4. Add the cooled rice to the skillet and turn the heat to high. Fry the rice with the vegetables for 5 minutes, stirring constantly.

5. Meanwhile, scramble the eggs: In a small skillet set over low heat, melt the butter. Add the eggs and cook until eggs just begin to set, 3 to 4 minutes.

6. Add the eggs, soy sauce, and fresh cilantro, and toss to incorporate.

7. Serve immediately.

UNTIL THE CHEESE BUBBLES VEGETARIAN LASAGNA

This is a massive vegetarian lasagna that will convert even the biggest meat-lovers in your life, or perhaps your favorite aunt, though we recommend making it one at a time and not in batches of a dozen. The gooey cheese in the pan might require a little extra scrubbing during clean-up—a little bonus fun for all you clean freaks out there.

Yield: 8 to 10 servings • *Prep time:* 45 minutes • *Cook time:* 45 minutes

1 (16-ounce) package dry lasagna noodles (not "no-boil")

2 tablespoons unsalted butter, divided

1 tablespoon olive oil

1 medium yellow onion, diced

1 large orange bell pepper, diced

1 medium zucchini, diced

3 cloves garlic, finely diced, divided

1½ teaspoons garlic powder

1½ teaspoons Italian seasoning

1½ teaspoons cumin

¼ cup shallots, finely diced (about 2 small shallots)

2 (17.6-ounce) cartons crushed tomatoes

1 tablespoon tomato paste

1 tablespoon brown sugar

8 ounces ricotta cheese

1 large egg, lightly beaten

24 ounces mozzarella cheese, grated

8 ounces Parmesan cheese, grated

fresh parsley, roughly chopped

salt and pepper, to taste

TO PREPARE THE LASAGNA:

1. Cook the lasagna noodles according to package instructions. Lay the cooked noodles on kitchen towels to dry.

2. In a medium skillet set over medium heat, melt 1 tablespoon of butter and drizzle in the olive oil. Add the diced onion and cook until slightly translucent, about 2 to 3 minutes. Add the bell pepper and cook for an additional 3 to 4 minutes, or until slightly tender. Add the zucchini and cook for another 3 to 4 minutes.

3. Reduce the heat to medium-low, add half of the garlic, and stir. Add the garlic powder, Italian seasoning, cumin, and salt and pepper. Remove from the heat and set aside.

4. In a small saucepan set over medium heat, melt the remaining tablespoon of butter. Add the shallots and cook until just beginning to turn translucent, 2 to 3 minutes. Add the remaining garlic and stir, being mindful not to burn it (reduce the heat to low if necessary). Pour in the crushed tomatoes, and add the tomato paste and brown sugar. Stir to incorporate, then let simmer for 10 minutes. Remove from the heat.

TO COMPLETE THE LASAGNA:

1. Preheat the oven to 400°F.

2. Spoon about ¼ cup of the tomato sauce over the bottom of a 9 x 13-inch baking dish.

3. Lay 3 or 4 lasagna noodles on the bottom of the baking dish. Spoon one-quarter of the ricotta mixture on top of the noodles, then spoon one-quarter of the vegetable mixture on top of that. Spoon about ¼ cup of the tomato sauce on top of this layer, then sprinkle some of the mozzarella and Parmesan. Repeat this step until you've layered the baking dish to the brim.

5. In a small bowl, stir the ricotta cheese and the egg to combine. Season with salt and pepper to taste.

4. Cover with aluminum foil and bake for 20 minutes.

5. Remove from the oven, discard the aluminum foil, and continue to bake uncovered for an additional 25 minutes, or until the lasagna is bubbly and the cheese has browned a bit on top.

6. Let cool for 30 minutes before cutting into the lasagna and serving it.

DESSERTS

ALL-OCCASION VANILLA CAKE

Here's a simple vanilla cake with whipped cream and fresh strawberries. Perfect for a birthday or really any occasion. Even introducing your dad to your new man-friend. Not awkward at all.

Yield: 12 servings • *Prep time:* 25 minutes • *Bake time:* 25 to 27 minutes

For the cake:

2 ¼ cups all-purpose flour

2 ¼ teaspoons baking powder

¾ teaspoon kosher salt

¾ cup (1 ½ sticks) unsalted butter, room temperature

1 ½ cups granulated sugar

3 large eggs, room temperature

1 ½ teaspoons vanilla extract

1 cup buttermilk, room temperature

For the whipped cream:

1 cup heavy whipping cream

1 tablespoon granulated sugar

1 teaspoon vanilla extract

For the topping:

1 package (16-ounces) fresh strawberries, sliced

TO MAKE THE CAKE:

1. Preheat the oven to 350°F.

2. Grease two 8-inch round cake pans with cooking spray, and line the bottom of each with parchment paper.

3. In a medium bowl, whisk together the flour, baking powder, and salt. Set aside.

4. In the bowl of a stand mixer set to medium speed or using a hand mixer, cream together the butter and sugar until very fluffy, about 3 minutes.

5. Crack in the eggs, one at a time and mix thoroughly after each addition. Add the vanilla and mix it in.

6. With the mixer set to low speed, add the flour mixture and the buttermilk in alternating batches. Make sure to begin and end with the flour mixture, and be mindful not to overmix the batter. Mix just until all ingredients are incorporated.

7. Divide the cake batter between the prepared pans and bake for 25 to 27 minutes, or until a toothpick inserted into the center comes out free of crumbs.

8. Let cool completely before making the whipped cream and decorating the cake.

TO MAKE THE WHIPPED CREAM:

1. Pour the heavy whipping cream into the bowl of a stand mixer or if using a hand mixer, in a medium mixing bowl. Add the sugar, and turn the mixer on high speed. Whip the cream until peaks form. If you prefer soft peaks, whip for about 5 minutes. For stiff peaks, whip for 7 to 8 minutes.

2. Once the cream is the consistency you prefer, drizzle in the vanilla extract and stir gently just to combine.

TO DECORATE THE CAKE:

1. Set one layer of the cake on a cake turntable and carefully slice off the dome or top of the cake. Spread half of the whipped cream on top of the cake, then arrange the strawberry slices on top of the whipped cream. If you don't have a cake turntable, simply set the first cake layer on a large cutting board and rotate cutting board as you frost.

2. Place the second layer of cake on top of the first, and repeat step 1.

3. Serve immediately.

MEMORABLE KIWI-LIME PIE

This is a great pie to make during hotter summer months. Just make sure none of your family or friends have a kiwi allergy, especially if they also have a slight phobia of needles.

Yield: 8 servings • *Prep time:* 10 minutes • *Bake time:* 25 minutes • *Chill time:* 8 hours

For the crust:

1¼ cups graham cracker crumbs (about 9 sheets of graham crackers)

2 tablespoons granulated sugar

5 tablespoons unsalted butter, melted

For the filling:

1 (14-ounce) can sweetened condensed milk

4 large egg yolks

½ cup plus 2 tablespoons bottled key lime juice

For the topping:

10 slices fresh kiwi

TO MAKE THE CRUST:

1. Preheat the oven to 350°F.

2. In a mixing bowl, stir the graham cracker crumbs, sugar, and melted butter with a fork just to combine. Press the crumbs into a 9-inch pie plate and bake for 10 minutes. Let cool slightly while making the filling.

TO MAKE THE FILLING:

1. In a medium bowl, whisk the sweetened condensed milk and egg yolks until combined. Add the key lime juice and mix well.

2. Pour the filling into the graham cracker crust and bake for 15 minutes.

3. Let the pie cool completely on a cooling rack (the filling will continue to set as it cools), then cover with plastic wrap and chill for at least 8 hours.

4. Top the pie with kiwi slices right before serving.

FUDGY CHOCOLATE BROWNIES

These brownies take just one bowl to make and exactly zero brown bags, empty or not. This recipe makes 18 brownies so even if you get hungry on the way to a date, there will be plenty more to share.

Yield: 18 brownies • *Prep time:* 10 minutes • *Bake time:* 30 minutes

¾ cup (1½ sticks) unsalted butter

1 (4-ounce) semi-sweet chocolate baking bar, roughly chopped

2 cups granulated sugar

3 large eggs, room temperature

2 teaspoons vanilla extract

1 cup unsweetened natural cocoa powder

1 cup all-purpose flour

1 teaspoon salt

1. Preheat the oven to 350°F.

2. Grease a 9 x 13-inch baking dish with cooking spray and line with parchment paper.

3. In either a microwave-safe bowl or in a small saucepan set over medium heat, melt the butter and 2 ounces of the chopped chocolate. Melt in 30 second increments if using a microwave. Whisk constantly until completely smooth if melting on the stovetop.

4. Whisk in the sugar until combined, then whisk in the eggs and vanilla extract.

5. Using a rubber spatula, fold the cocoa powder, flour, salt, and remaining 2 ounces of chocolate into the wet ingredients until very well combined. The batter will be thick.

6. Spread the batter into the prepared baking dish. Bake for 30 minutes, or until a toothpick inserted into the center comes out mostly clean (a few crumbs are fine).

7. Let cool completely on a cooling rack before cutting into squares.

"FRENCH AUNT" CHOCOLATE CHIP COOKIES

This is a truly classic and delicious chocolate chip cookie. The recipe is from the back of a popular company's chocolate chip bag and definitely not from anyone's "French" aunt. You no longer need to experiment with tons of different recipes to find the perfect one!

Yield: 5 dozen cookies • *Prep time:* 10 minutes • *Bake time:* 9 to 11 minutes

2¼ cups all-purpose flour

1 teaspoon baking soda

1 teaspoon salt

1 cup (2 sticks) unsalted butter, room temperature

¾ cup granulated sugar

¾ cup light brown sugar

2 large eggs

1 teaspoon vanilla extract

2 cups Nestle Toll House Semi-Sweet Chocolate Morsels

1 cup nuts (your preference), chopped (optional)

1. Preheat the oven to 375°F.

2. Line a baking sheet with parchment paper.

3. In a medium bowl, gently whisk the flour, baking soda, and salt just to combine. Set aside.

4. In the bowl of a stand mixer set to medium speed, or using a hand mixer, cream the butter for 1 minute. Add both sugars and continue to cream until light and fluffy, about 2 minutes. Crack in the eggs, add the vanilla, and mix to combine.

5. Add the dry ingredients to the wet ingredients and mix on low.

6. Fold in the chocolate chips and nuts, if using, by hand using a rubber spatula.

7. Drop by rounded tablespoon onto the prepared baking sheet.

8. Bake for 9 to 11 minutes, or until the edges have begun to crisp and the cookies are golden brown.

9. Let cool on the baking sheet for 1 minute, then transfer to a cooling rack.

DIVORCED PARENTS PUMPKIN PIE

Even the best-laid holiday plans can go awry when divorce or runaway balloons get in the mix. No matter if the potatoes aren't lumpy enough or the turkey dries out, any meal that ends with this delicious pumpkin pie will be a happy one. It's so good, it might even heal the hurts leftover from your parents' break up.

Yield: 8 servings • *Prep time:* 5 minutes • *Bake time:* 50 to 55 minutes

For the whipped cream:
½ cup heavy whipping cream
1 tablespoon granulated sugar

For the pumpkin pie:
1 (15-ounce) can pumpkin puree
1 (14-ounce) can sweetened condensed milk
2 large eggs
1 teaspoon ground cinnamon
½ teaspoon ground nutmeg
½ teaspoon salt
1 (9-inch) frozen pie crust

TO MAKE THE WHIPPED CREAM:

In the bowl of a stand mixer set to medium-high speed, or using a hand mixer, whip the heavy cream and sugar until stiff peaks form, 6 to 7 minutes. Let chill in the refrigerator until ready to use.

TO MAKE THE PIE:

1. Preheat the oven to 425°F.

2. In a medium bowl, whisk together the pumpkin puree, sweetened condensed milk, eggs, ground cinnamon, ground nutmeg, and salt until thoroughly combined.

3. Pour the mixture into the unbaked crust and bake for 15 minutes.

4. Reduce the temperature to 350°F and continue to bake for an additional 35 to 40 minutes. Remove from the oven and let cool completely before serving with whipped cream.

PERFECT POX PEACH COBBLER

Here's a great peach cobbler for the warmer summer months, or perhaps when you are recovering from chicken pox; it's delicious topped with ice cream. Hopefully this will be yummy enough to distract you from the scratching.

Yield: 10 servings • *Prep time:* 25 minutes • *Bake time:* 47 minutes

For the peach filling:

8 medium peaches, pitted and diced into 2-inch chunks

¼ cup light brown sugar

1 tablespoon cornstarch

½ tablespoon lemon zest

1 tablespoon freshly squeezed lemon juice (about ½ lemon)

½ teaspoon vanilla extract

½ teaspoon ground cinnamon

pinch of salt

For the biscuit topping:

2 cups all-purpose flour

½ cup granulated sugar

1 ½ teaspoons baking powder

¼ teaspoon baking soda

½ teaspoon salt

½ cup (1 stick) unsalted butter, cold and cubed

½ cup buttermilk

Egg wash:
1 large egg
splash of water

TO MAKE THE PEACH FILLING:

1. Preheat the oven to 350°F.

2. Grease a 9 x 13-inch baking dish with cooking spray.

3. In a large bowl, stir together the peaches, brown sugar, cornstarch, lemon zest, lemon juice, vanilla extract, ground cinnamon, and salt to combine.

4. Pour into the prepared baking dish, and bake for 7 minutes. Remove from the oven, but leave the heat on while preparing the biscuit topping.

TO MAKE THE BISCUIT TOPPING:

1. In a large bowl, whisk the flour, sugar, baking powder, baking soda, and salt to combine. Toss in the cold, cubed butter and stir with a rubber spatula, just to coat the butter with the flour. Using either two knives, a pastry cutter, or your fingers, work the butter into the dry ingredients until the butter is pea sized (some larger pieces are fine).

2. Stir in the buttermilk until it is incorporated.

3. Place handfuls of dough on top of the filling until the peaches are mostly covered.

TO COMPLETE THE COBBLER:

1. For the egg wash, beat the egg with a splash of water. Brush the tops of the biscuits with the wash. Return the baking dish to the oven and bake for another 40 minutes, or until a toothpick inserted into the center of the biscuit topping comes out clean and free of crumbs.

2. Let cool for 5 minutes before serving. (Try topping the cobbler with vanilla ice cream.)

BEST OATMEAL RAISIN COOKIES EVER

Should your friend's Italian boyfriend ever hit on you, you can try to mend the issue with these soft and chewy oatmeal raisin cookies.

Yield: 2 dozen cookies • *Prep time:* 30 minutes • *Bake time:* 11 to 13 minutes • *Chill time:* 30 minutes

1 ½ cups all-purpose flour

1 teaspoon baking soda

1 ½ teaspoons ground cinnamon

½ teaspoon salt

1 cup (2 sticks) unsalted butter, softened

1 cup light brown sugar

2 large eggs, room temperature

½ tablespoon vanilla extract

1 tablespoon molasses

3 cups old-fashioned rolled oats

1 cup raisins

1. In a medium mixing bowl, whisk the flour, baking soda, ground cinnamon, and salt to combine. Set aside.

2. Using either a stand or hand mixer, cream the butter and sugar on medium speed until very light and fluffy, about 3 minutes. Add the eggs and continue to mix until combined, about 1 minute. Scrape down the sides of the bowl with a rubber spatula as needed. Add the vanilla extract and molasses, and mix to combine thoroughly.

3. With the mixer set to low speed, add the dry ingredients to the wet ingredients and mix until just barely combined.

4. Using a rubber spatula, fold in the oats and raisins. The dough will be thick and sticky. Cover the mixing bowl with plastic wrap and place in the refrigerator for 30 minutes.

5. Remove the chilled dough and preheat the oven to 350°F.

6. Line a baking sheet with parchment paper. Roll balls of dough (about 2 tablespoons each) and place them 2 inches apart on the baking sheet.

7. Bake for 11 to 13 minutes, or until the cookies just begin to brown around the edges. The cookies will look soft and not quite done baking, but they will continue to bake from residual heat in the baking sheet as they cool.

8. Cool on the baking sheet for 5 minutes, then transfer to a cooling rack to cool completely before serving.

FAKE CHOCOLATE CAKE WITH CRANBERRY FROSTING

A moist faux-chocolate cake made with carob (which is tastier than you might imagine) will satisfy even the most devoted chocolate lovers.

Yield: 12 servings • *Prep time:* 25 minutes • *Cook time:* 35 to 52 minutes

For the cranberry jam:

1 cup fresh or frozen cranberries, sliced in half

4 tablespoons granulated sugar

4 tablespoons water

For the cake:

1¾ cups all-purpose flour

1¾ cups granulated sugar

¼ cup carob powder

1 teaspoon baking powder

2 teaspoons baking soda

1 teaspoon salt

1 cup buttermilk, room temperature

2 large eggs, room temperature

½ cup vegetable oil

1 teaspoon vanilla extract

1 cup freshly brewed hot coffee

For the buttercream:

1¼ cups (2½ sticks) unsalted butter, softened

⅓ cup cranberry jam

3–4 cups confectioners' sugar

3–4 tablespoons heavy cream or full-fat milk

1 teaspoon vanilla extract

pinch of salt

TO MAKE THE JAM:

In a small saucepan set over medium heat, add the cranberries, sugar, and water, and bring to a gentle boil. After about 5 minutes, reduce heat to medium-low, and continue to cook cranberry mixture until it has thickened, 5 to 10 minutes more. Remove from heat and let cool while you make the rest of the cake.

TO MAKE THE CAKE:

1. Preheat the oven to 350°F.

2. Grease two 9-inch cake pans with cooking spray and line the bottoms with parchment paper.

3. In a medium bowl, whisk the flour, sugar, carob, baking powder, baking soda, and salt to combine.

4. In a large bowl, whisk the buttermilk, eggs, vegetable oil, and vanilla extract to combine.

5. Slowly pour the dry ingredients into the wet ingredients. Whisk slowly until the batter is thoroughly combined. Pour in the hot coffee and whisk very slowly until batter is thoroughly incorporated (batter will be thin).

6. Pour the batter into the prepared cake pans and bake for 25 to 27 minutes, or until a toothpick inserted into the center comes out mostly free of crumbs.

7. Let cake cool in the cake pans for 5 minutes. Run a butter knife around the edges of the cake to remove from cake pan. Transfer cakes to a cooling rack to cool completely before frosting.

TO MAKE THE BUTTERCREAM:

1. In the bowl stand mixer set to medium speed or using a hand mixer, cream the butter until fluffy, about 3 minutes. Add the cranberry jam and mix to incorporate. The mixture may look curdled at this point, but it will come together when you add the confectioners' sugar.

2. Add the confectioners' sugar 1 cup at a time on low speed to combine. Pour in the heavy cream or milk, vanilla extract, and salt.

3. Mix on low speed until the buttercream is the desired consistency.

TO DECORATE THE CAKE:

1. Using a serrated knife, level off the tops of the cake layers. Spread ⅓ cup of the buttercream on the top layer with an offset spatula or butter knife. Spread the buttercream evenly and just to the edge of the cake.

2. Place the second layer on top of the first, and repeat step 1.

3. Spread the remaining buttercream on the sides of the cake, then chill for 30 minutes before slicing and serving.

CHRISTMAS CARAMEL CANDIES

These delightful caramels are good enough to give to all your neighbors, who may even line up outside your door for them! Christmas caramel—now that would be perfection!

Yield: 20 candies • *Prep time:* 15 minutes • *Cook time:* 45 minutes
• *Chill time:* 1 to 8 hours

2 cups apple cider vinegar
4 tablespoons (½ stick) unsalted butter
½ cup granulated sugar
¼ cup light brown sugar

3 tablespoons heavy cream
¼ teaspoon ground cinnamon
¾ teaspoon kosher salt

1. Grease a 9 x 5 x 3-inch baking dish with cooking spray, then line the bottom with parchment paper.

2. In a large saucepan set over high heat, reduce the apple cider to about ¼ cup, about 30 minutes.

3. Once the apple cider has reduced, add the butter, both sugars, and the heavy cream. Cook until the mixture registers 255°F degrees on a candy thermometer, about 15 minutes.

4. Immediately stir in the ground cinnamon and salt, and pour into the prepared pan. Let the candy chill and set in the refrigerator for at least 1 hour or up to overnight. Using a small paring knife, slice into individual caramel candies.

5. If the candies will be used as holiday gifts, wrap them in candy wax papers.

FABULOUS FLAN

A festive Mexican custard dessert is not just good—it's flan-tastic. And this recipe is good enough to have in lieu of birthday cake, even if the rest of the food committee prefers something a little less... gooey.

Yield: 6 servings • *Prep time:* 20 minutes • *Cook time:* 55 minutes • *Chill time:* 8 hours

1¾ cups heavy whipping cream
1 cup whole milk
pinch of salt
½ vanilla bean, split lengthwise

1 cup plus 7 tablespoons granulated sugar
⅓ cup water
3 large eggs
2 large egg yolks

1. Preheat the oven to 350°F.

2. In a medium saucepan set over medium heat, combine the heavy whipping cream, milk, and salt. Scrape the vanilla bean seeds into the saucepan, add the bean pod as well, and bring to a simmer, about 4 minutes. Once the liquid is gently simmering, remove from the heat and let steep for 30 minutes.

3. While the mixture is steeping, make the caramel by combining 1 cup of sugar and the water in another medium saucepan. Stir over low heat until the sugar dissolves. Increase the heat to high and cook (don't stir but simply swirl the pan from time to time) until the syrup is deep golden amber, about 10 to 12 minutes. Quickly but carefully pour the caramel into six ¾-cup ramekins. Tilt each ramekin on its side to distribute the caramel up the sides of the cup. Place all six ramekins into a 9 x 13-inch baking dish.

4. In a medium bowl, whisk the whole eggs and egg yolks, then slowly pour in the 7 tablespoons of sugar. Gently whisk the reserved cream mixture into the egg mixture. Pour through a small sieve, then distribute evenly into the prepared ramekins.

5. Pour enough hot water into the baking dish to come halfway up the sides of the ramekins. Bake until the flan centers are softly set, about 40 minutes. Transfer the ramekins to a cooling rack.

6. Cover and chill overnight.

7. To serve, run a small sharp knife around the edge of each ramekin and turn over onto a small serving plate. Drizzle with the leftover caramel from the ramekins.

CHOCOLATE MOUSSE

In case your date's dessert order has you in the mood for homemade chocolate mousse, this recipe will satisfy your cravings. You'll probably never get a second date, but at least you get the mousse to yourself.

Yield: 8 servings • *Prep time:* 15 minutes • *Chill time:* 2 hours

4 large egg yolks
¼ cup granulated sugar
2½ cups heavy whipping cream, divided

6 ounces semi-sweet chocolate chips
raspberries, to serve

1. In the bowl of a stand mixer set to high speed or using a hand mixer, mix the egg yolks until thickened slightly, about 3 minutes. Pour in the sugar and mix on medium speed just until combined. Set aside.

2. In a medium saucepan set over medium heat, add 1 cup of the heavy cream. Heat just until warmed through, 1 to 2 minutes. Gradually add half of the heated heavy cream into the egg mixture and stir just to combine.

3. Pour the egg and heavy cream mixture back into the saucepan, and whisk constantly over high heat for 5 minutes, or until the mixture thickens slightly. Be careful not to bring it to a boil.

4. Using a wooden spoon, stir in the chocolate chips until melted. Remove from the heat, cover with plastic wrap, and chill in the refrigerator for 2 hours, stirring occasionally.

5. After chilling, pour the remaining heavy cream into the bowl of a stand mixer or a medium mixing bowl if using a hand mixer. With the mixer set to high speed, beat until soft peaks form, 6 to 7 minutes. Fold the chilled chocolate mixture into the whipped cream, being gentle and mindful not to deflate the mousse.

6. Either spoon or pipe the mousse into individual dessert cups to serve. Top with fresh raspberries.

THANKSGIVING TRIFLE

The shredded coconut in here is meant to represent the ground beef in a shepherd's pie—should you accidentally combine two different Thanksgiving recipes into one! Don't worry, your friends will love this dessert and no one will complain that it tastes like feet.

Yield: 4 to 6 servings • *Prep time:* 25 minutes • *Chill time:* 1 to 8 hours

1 cup heavy whipping cream

2 cups instant vanilla pudding (half of a 3.4-ounce box)

1½ cups unsweetened shredded coconut

6 tablespoons chocolate hazelnut spread

24 ounces pound cake, cut into ½-inch cubes

½ cup seedless raspberry jam

24 ounces fresh raspberries, washed and dried

fresh mint springs (optional)

TO MAKE THE TRIFLE:

l. Into the bowl of a stand mixer set to high speed, or using a hand mixer, pour the heavy cream. Mix on high speed until soft peaks form, 6 to 7 minutes. Cover the bowl with plastic wrap and chill in the refrigerator while you continue making the trifle.

2. Prepare the instant vanilla pudding according to package instructions. Refrigerate while you continue with the recipe.

TO ASSEMBLE THE TRIFLE:

1. Place about half of the pound cake in a 7½-inch glass trifle dish or a large glass bowl. Spoon about half of the raspberry jam on top of the pound cake and spread using an offset spatula or butter knife.

2. Spoon half of the vanilla pudding on top of the jam, then top with a layer of the coconut and chocolate hazelnut mixture. Spoon about half of the whipped cream

3. In a small mixing bowl, stir the coconut and chocolate hazelnut spread to combine. Set aside.

on top of the coconut and chocolate hazelnut. Top this layer with half of the fresh raspberries.

3. Repeat with the remaining ingredients, to the brim of the dish.

4. Let chill in the refrigerator for at least 1 hour and up to 8 hours.

5. Top with fresh mint sprigs, if desired, right before serving.

FLOOR CHEESECAKE

This cheesecake is so good, you'll be willing to cheat, lie, or steal for it. Just as long as you don't resort to eating it off the floor.... Ideas for cheesecake toppings are caramel, chocolate or berry sauce, and whipped cream.

Yield: 8 to 12 servings • *Prep time:* 10 minutes • *Cook time:* 68 minutes
• *Chill time:* 8 hours

For the graham cracker crust:

1½ cups graham cracker crumbs (about 9 sheets of graham crackers)

5 tablespoons unsalted butter, melted

¼ cup granulated sugar

For the cheesecake:

4 (8-ounce) blocks full-fat cream cheese, softened

1 cup, plus 2 tablespoons granulated sugar

1 cup full-fat sour cream, room temperature

1½ teaspoons vanilla extract, divided

juice of 1 small lemon

3 large eggs, room temperature

1. Preheat the oven to 350°F. Grease a 9-inch springform pan with cooking spray and set aside.

2. Pour the graham cracker crumbs into a medium mixing bowl, add the melted butter and ¼ cup sugar, and stir to combine with a rubber spatula. Press the graham cracker crust mixture into the bottom and slightly up the sides of the prepared springform pan.

3. Prebake the crust for 8 minutes, remove from the oven, and place on a large sheet of aluminum foil. Allow to cool slightly.

4. In the bowl of a stand mixer set to medium speed or using a hand mixer, cream together the cream cheese and sugar until the mixture is smooth and creamy. Add the sour cream, vanilla extract, and lemon juice, and mix until thoroughly combined. Add the eggs, one at a time, and mix well after each addition but be mindful not to overmix.

5. To make a water bath, boil a medium pot of water. While the water is boiling, wrap the aluminum foil around the sides of the springform pan. Pour the cheesecake batter on top of the graham cracker crust, using a rubber spatula to spread the mixture evenly.

6. Place the springform pan inside a large roasting pan. Carefully pour the boiled water about an inch up the sides of the roasting pan. Place in the oven and bake for 55 to 60 minutes, or until the center of the cheesecake is nearly set. Remove from oven and set aside while you make the frosting.

7. In a small mixing bowl, whisk the sour cream, remaining sugar, and vanilla until well blended; carefully spread over cheesecake. Bake cheesecake for an additional 10 minutes, or until the frosting has set.

8. Turn the oven off, but leave the cheesecake inside and open the oven door slightly. Let the cheesecake cool down inside the oven for 1 hour. Remove and let cool at room temperature.

9. Refrigerate for at least 4 hours or up to 8 hours before slicing and serving.

MAD, SAD, AND GLAD CHOCOLATE DONUTS

Many food fanatics would probably like to thank a certain '90s television sitcom starring six best friends for introducing them to the phrase "round food for every mood." The phrase is as hilarious as these cake donuts are delicious.

Yield: 8 donuts • *Prep time:* 10 minutes • *Bake time:* 10 minutes

For the donuts:

1 cup all-purpose flour

1 teaspoon baking powder

¼ teaspoon baking soda

¼ teaspoon ground nutmeg

1 large egg, room temperature

⅓ cup light brown sugar

¼ cup whole milk, room temperature

¼ cup full-fat Greek yogurt

2 tablespoons unsalted butter, melted

1½ teaspoons vanilla extract

½ cup rainbow sprinkles

For the chocolate glaze:

1½ cups confectioners' sugar

4 tablespoons natural cocoa powder

2 tablespoons full-fat milk

2 teaspoons vanilla extract

TO MAKE THE DONUTS:

1. Preheat the oven to 350°F. Grease a donut pan with cooking spray.

2. In a medium mixing bowl, whisk the flour, baking powder, baking soda, and ground nutmeg to combine.

3. In another medium mixing bowl, whisk the egg, brown sugar, milk, Greek yogurt, melted butter, and vanilla extract to incorporate.

4. Pour the wet ingredients into the flour mixture. Using a rubber spatula, stir to incorporate. The batter will be thick.

5. Transfer the batter to a pastry bag and fill each cavity in the donut pan about three-quarters full. You can also simply spoon the donut batter into each donut cavity.

6. Bake for 10 minutes, or until the edges are lightly browned. Transfer to a cooling rack and let cool slightly before glazing.

TO MAKE THE CHOCOLATE GLAZE:

1. In a small mixing bowl, whisk all ingredients until smooth and completely incorporated.

2. Pour rainbow sprinkles in a small bowl.

3. Dip the top of each donut into the glaze, then dip in the rainbow sprinkles.

4. Return to the cooling rack to set.

DRINKS

THE CAPE CODDER

Take a big shot of vodka and add a bit of cranberry to make this tasty classic cocktail that one of your best friend's outspoken Italian sisters might enjoy on occasion. Make sure to drink responsibly so you can remember which sister.

Yield: 1 serving • *Prep time:* 1 minute

3 ounces cranberry juice
2 ounces vodka

juice of ½ a lime
lime wedges, for garnish

1. Fill a highball glass to the brim with ice. Pour cranberry juice and vodka over ice and stir well.

2. Squeeze the juice from the lime and garnish with lime wedges.

NO-FAUX HOT CHOCOLATE

Use any brand of unsweetened cocoa powder for this hot chocolate topped with whipped cream to share with a friend. You can try it with carob powder, but you know what can happen when you substitute a critical ingredient…. The recipe can easily be increased or reduced to accommodate any number of friends.

Yield: 2 servings • *Prep time:* 9 minutes • *Cook time:* 4 minutes

For the hot chocolate:

2 cups whole milk

2 tablespoons granulated sugar

2 tablespoons unsweetened cocoa powder

1 teaspoon vanilla extract

For the whipped cream:

½ cup heavy whipping cream

1 tablespoon granulated sugar

Toppings (optional):

chocolate chips

dusting of cocoa powder

TO MAKE THE HOT CHOCOLATE:

1. Heat the milk, sugar, cocoa powder, and vanilla extract in small saucepan over medium heat, and whisk continuously until chocolate has dissolved.

2. Pour into mugs right before you are ready to serve, then top with a dollop of whipped cream and, if desired, additional toppings.

TO MAKE THE WHIPPED CREAM:

In the bowl of a stand mixer set to medium-high speed, or using a hand mixer, whip the heavy cream and sugar until stiff peaks form, 6 to 7 minutes.

NOT-SO-FINE MARGARITAS

If you ever find out the love of your life is dating one of your best friends, you'll find a little liquid therapy in this margarita recipe. Each batch gets better and better, and they will help cut any weirdness or tension that is definitely (not) in the room.

Yield: 4 to 6 servings • *Prep time:* 5 minutes

2 tablespoons kosher salt

1½ cups blanco tequila

¾ cup fresh lime juice (from about 5–6 small limes)

2 tablespoons superfine sugar

4–6 lime slices

1. Pour kosher salt onto a small plate. Rub 1 lime wedge around the rim of each serving glass. Tip each glass into the salt to coat the lip of the glasses. Set aside.

2. In a large pitcher, add the tequila, fresh lime juice, and superfine sugar. Stir with a spoon to combine.

3. Add enough ice to the pitcher to fill about half-way. Pour margaritas into prepared serving glasses and garnish each with the remaining lime wedges.

CEILING BANANA SMOOTHIE

Clean that banana smoothie that got on your ceiling after your friend told you she was breaking up with her boyfriend—your brother—and make this one instead.

Yield: 2 servings • *Prep time:* 5 minutes

1 medium banana, halved

½ medium orange, peeled and quartered

⅓ cup full-fat Greek yogurt

¼ cup whole milk

2 teaspoons honey

1. Add the banana, orange, Greek yogurt, and milk to a blender. Blend until creamy and smooth.

2. Drizzle in the honey and blend just a few seconds more.

3. Serve immediately.

SPICED CIDER

Properly label your cooking fat to save your friend from mistaking it for this delicious spiced cider. Unless drinking a glass of fat is your idea of a great apology, of course.

Yield: 12 servings • *Prep time:* 5 minutes • *Cook time:* 3 hours

10 sweet apples, such as Gala, quartered

¾ cup granulated sugar

1 tablespoon ground cinnamon

1 tablespoon ground nutmeg

1. To a large stockpot set over medium heat, add the apples and enough water to cover by 2 inches.

2. Stir in the sugar and spices, and bring to a rolling boil.

3. Boil uncovered for 1 hour.

4. Cover the pot, reduce the heat, and simmer for an additional 2 hours.

5. Strain the mixture through a fine mesh sieve and discard the solids. Strain the cider a second time and serve cider warm.

FUN IRISH COFFEE

Here's an Irish coffee to meet all your (morning) cocktail needs. Let's hope this brings out the Fun in you and your friends. But be careful—too many of these and you might find yourself dancing around like Michael Flatley, Lord of the Dance!

Yield: 6 servings • *Prep time:* 6 minutes

½ cup heavy whipping cream

36 ounces freshly brewed coffee, about 6 cups

4 teaspoons granulated sugar

2 teaspoons light brown sugar

6 ounces Irish whiskey

1. In the bowl of a stand mixer set to high speed or using a hand mixer, whip the heavy cream for 5 to 6 minutes until soft peaks form. Refrigerate until ready to serve.

2. Pour the brewed coffee into a medium pitcher. Add the granulated and brown sugars and stir until fully dissolved.

3. Pour the coffee into 6 coffee cups, and top off each with 1 ounce of whiskey.

4. Top each cup with a dollop of whipped cream and serve immediately.

TIKI DEATH PUNCH

Whether you get your girlfriends together for a backyard barbecue or weekend slumber party, this two-rum tiki punch is so good that your friends will slurp it down before you can even recite all the ingredients. Pairs well with cookie dough and deep contemplation of your life plan.

Yield: 6 servings • *Prep time:* 5 minutes • *Chill time:* 2 hours

3 cups frozen fruit punch
½ cup coconut-flavored rum
¼ cup pineapple-flavored rum
juice of 1 lemon

juice of 1 large navel orange
1 cup lemon-lime soda
pineapple and orange slices, for garnish

1. Add the fruit punch, two rums, lemon juice, and orange juice to a large pitcher, and stir to blend.

2. Chill in the refrigerator for at least 2 hours.

3. Stir in the lemon-lime soda right before serving.

4. Serve over ice, and garnish with pineapple and orange slices.

VACAY MIMOSAS

You can definitely have a mimosa for breakfast, whether you are actually on vacation or not. Just maybe don't have too many while you're discussing your best friend's (most recent) divorce.

Yield: 4 servings • *Prep time:* 5 minutes

2 whole large navel oranges, thinly sliced into half-moons

3 cups freshly squeezed or bottled orange juice

1 (750mL) bottle champagne or prosecco

1. Place the orange half-moons into a large pitcher.

2. Pour the orange juice into the pitcher, and top with the bottle of champagne or prosecco.

3. Serve in champagne glasses over ice, if desired.

STRAWBERRY MILKSHAKE

A strawberry milkshake so good, it deserves to be on a TV show's promotional poster. This recipe makes four servings, but it's way more fun to drink a giant one with multiple straws!

Yield: 4 servings • *Prep time:* 5 minutes

8 ounces strawberries, hulled and sliced
½ teaspoon vanilla extract
1 pint strawberry ice cream, softened

1 cup full-fat milk
mint, to serve

1. Place all ingredients into a blender and blend on high until smooth and creamy, about 2 minutes. Pour into 4 milkshake glasses, or tall drinking glasses. Top with mint, if desired.

2. Serve immediately.

PHOTO CREDITS

● ● ●

ABOUT THE AUTHOR

Teresa Finney is a food writer, recipe developer, baker, and lover of '90s television originally from the San Francisco Bay Area. She's now based in Atlanta, Georgia. You can follow her on Twitter at @teresaafinney or on Instagram at @milagrokitchen.